BEHOLD HIS GLORY!

BEHOLD HIS GLORY!

A Testament of God's Healing Power
and of His Eternal Love, Protection, and Deliverance

Evangelist Jacqueline Stevenson
Minister of the Gospel of Jesus Christ
Dedicated Wife and Mother

RBH Professional Publishing
Southfield, Michigan

Copyright © 2019 by Evangelist Jacqueline Stevenson

All Rights Reserved. No part of this book may be used or reproduced in any manner without the express written permission of the author, except in the brief quotations of scriptural references from the Bible. For information on use of materials and content contained herein, send requests to gloriousinspirations7@hotmail.com or permissions@rbhprofessionalpublishing.com

RBH Professional Publishing, a division of RBH Professional Development Institute
Southfield, Michigan 48075
www.rbhprofessionalpublishing.com

Printed in the United States of America
Library of Congress Cataloging-in-Publication Data
Library of Congress Control Number:2019913828

ISBN 978-1-7339533-2-0
eISBN 978-1-7339533-3-7

Edited by R. L. Stevenson

Cover Book Design: R.L. Stevenson

Front Cover Graphic Image:
Courtesy of Adobe Spark Royalty Free Graphics

Dedication

This book is dedicated to the memory of my beloved Sister…
Genevieve Pamela Springer

~ And ~

…Unto God (for His Faithfulness).

Special Dedication

To my precious parents, the late Willard Frederick. Sr., and Mary Rosalie Springer – Thank you for being wonderful examples, and for rearing my siblings and me in the fear and admonition of the Lord.

To all of my other beloved siblings: Carol (deceased); Shirley; Marion; Bernice (deceased); Willard Frederick, Jr.; Douglas; the twins-Curtis & Cecil; and Rosalie; and to ALL of my nieces and nephews (on both sides of the family) – I love you with all of my heart and hope this work inspires and encourages you in the Lord.

Acknowledgments

I would like to first thank My Lord and Savior, Jesus Christ, from Whom all blessings flow. Thank you for showing your hand so mightily in my life, and in the lives of those near and dear to me. You are my love, peace, joy, and strength!

To the love of my life, my earthly companion for 53 years, my dear husband, Walter Lewis Stevenson, Sr. Only you know more than I do, the many challenges we have faced, and the level of commitment, desire, and strength it took for us to overcome. Our faith and trust in Christ is the sole reason the words in this book have come to LIGHT. We have witnessed the Power and Majesty of God, together, and I thank you for being there with me through it all.

To my posterity, my 12 children, Eld. Walter Lewis, Jr.; Eld. Tracy Alexander; Alan Raynard; Lawrence Anthony; Marlena Elaine; Rochelle Lanette; Jacquelyn Renee (J-Renee); Melanie Elise; Min. Rodrick Wesley and his wife, my daughter-in-law, Lij; Erica Celeste; Lisa Colleen; and Francine Regina (my miracle baby) –

Thank you for being instrumentally used by our Creator to show forth His glorious healing power through you, by my hands, and for being so very enthusiastic in encouraging me to write this memoir. Thank you for pressing me to get the job done! Remain steadfast and unmovable, always abounding in the work of the Lord. I love you all!

To my grandchildren, Ashley; Walter Lewis, III; Joseph; Jamal; Tyler; Lauryn; Victor; Da'Jah; Alexis; Leyah; Brea; Alayah; Daniel David, Jr.; Lauryel; Isabelle (Izzy); Rodrick-Josiah (RJ); and to my first great-grandchild, Londyn Lauryel:

In all that you do, do as unto the Lord, remembering Him always, keeping His Will in your hearts, always walking in the fear and admonition of Him, and in the Love of our Lord and Savior, Jesus Christ.

Be ye thankful and give God Praise for all of the Wonderful and Mighty Things He has done, and for all that He will continue to do in your lives; for He is Faithful, Just, and True!

This book serves as a Testament of His Faithfulness and of the Wondrous and Mighty Acts of Healing and Deliverance in our family!

Hallelujah! Hallelujah! Hallelujah!

Special Recognition

To my wonderful grandson, Walter, III – for being more than willing to spend countless hours deciphering and transcribing my notes and bringing forth the first electronic copy of the manuscript. I thank you for your diligence and enthusiasm, and for your appreciation of the written work as you carefully transcribed my thoughts…that was so very encouraging to me!

To my very diligent and insightful second eldest daughter, Rochelle Lanette – I know you expressed that you need no honorable mention or acknowledgment, but your brother and I insisted! (Smiles) Thank you for vigilantly considering my vision for the book and for carefully designing the theme and cover, for completing the digital manuscript, and for taking on the tedious and painstaking task of editing the work. I truly appreciate you for preserving my voice, and for contributing details about the testimonies mentioned in this memoir.

Special, Special Acknowledgment
To my faithful, helpful, and caring eldest son, Walter, Jr. (Co-Editor and Contributor *Mom's Surgery*) – From your youth, you have been a constant helper in countless ways, in so many instances…too many to name throughout your life, without question. I especially thank you for orchestrating and supervising every detail surrounding my critical stay in the hospital, before and after my surgery, along with the intimate excerpts regarding your steps in navigating the healing process, at the leading of the Lord, that have been penned in this memoir. Also, thank you for networking and for recommending the publisher, Regina Hall—RBH Professional Publishing, and for connecting me with Evang. LouAnne Lucas, who helped to facilitate my initial book launch. I certainly look forward to the plethora of

other opportunities (soon to come). You have truly been my right arm, and I am so pleased!

To my fifth eldest daughter (my 10th eldest child), Erica Celeste – Thank you so much, Cokie, for helping me during such a critical and trying time. I am tremendously grateful, that during my recovery after the surgery, the Lord placed me in the care of one of the most capable caregivers and nurturers He has gifted to the world. Keep up the blessed work, sweetheart!

To my faithful cousin, Gwendolyn Burns – Ever since we were children, you've always been more than loving and supportive, full of encouraging words, and always such delightful company whenever we're together. I appreciate you for staying connected – your fellowship has always meant so much! Much love, always!

To my wonderful and loving in-laws, Odessa, Samuel (Sam) and Jerice, and Yvonne – Words cannot express how deeply grateful I am for such loving, thoughtful, kind, and Godly wise in-laws. You've always shown genuine concern for me…I love you dearly!

To Evangelist LouAnne Lucas, thank you for being so genuinely sweet and encouraging. I appreciate your support…you are truly endearing and inspirational!

To my dearest, lifelong friends, Ola and Willeda – We've known each other since 7th grade and have continued to strengthen our sisterhood and camaraderie for nearly 60 years! I look forward to our annual get-togethers on those very special occasions. Thank you for always being there!

Finally, many thanks to Dr. Regina Banks-Hall and her publishing team for accepting the work, and for getting it print-ready. I truly appreciate you for your professionalism and expertise in bringing the finished product into fruition.

TO GOD BE THE GLORY FOR ALL OF THE WONDERFUL THINGS HE HAS DONE, AND FOR EVERY NEW THING YET TO COME!

"EYES HAVE NOT SEEN, NOR HAVE EARS HEARD, NEITHER HAS IT ENTERED INTO THE HEART OF MAN, THE THINGS THAT GOD HAS IN STORE FOR [US]."

HALLELUJAH AND AMEN!

Evangelist Jackie Stevenson

CONTENTS

Preface xv
Introduction 1
The Dedication 2
Childhood Memories 6

Miracles Upon Miracles! 13
    Miracle (1): *Salvation* 15
    Miracle (2): In-filling of the Holy Spirit 17
    Miracle (3): Beyond Conception 21
    Miracle (4): Beyond the Shadow of Doubt 22
    Miracle (5): By the Word of Faith 24
    Miracle (6): Rain Down Healing on Us 26
    Miracle (7): My Miracle Baby 28
    Miracle (8): Restoration of Life 32
    Miracle (9): Irene's Deliverance 34
    Miracle (10): God's Undeniable Handiwork 37
    Miracle (11): Confirmation in a Dream 40
    Miracle (12): "No Good Thing Will He Withhold…" 41

The Dream 44
The Paper – (ca. December 2, 1998) 46
The Savior's Date of Birth 48

Miracles upon Miracles – (Part 2) 55
    Miracle (13): An Elder's Deliverance 57
    Miracle (14) – The Surgery 59

    Walter's Testimony: A Miracle from the Lord!.................................. 61
    Miracle (15): My Hubby's Dilemma.. 67

The Dream of March 1979 69
"Proclaim and Declare" 71
    Miracle (16): God's Word Confirmed 75
    Miracle (17): Testimony of One Healed 76
    Miracle (18): Delivered…Unexpectedly!.. 77
    Miracle (19): The Thief Cometh… But, God!.................................... 79
    Miracle (20): Seven from Heaven!.. 81
    Miracle (21): Thank God for Her Deliverance!................................. 82

From the Author…. 85

PREFACE

The testimonies in this book show forth the great power and glory of God Almighty. There are no words, I believe, that exist in any vernacular, adequate enough, or that can fully express, the magnitude of His wondrous majesty, and of my eternal gratitude toward Him!

Every occurrence contained and expressed herein is 100% authentic, and all of the glory belongs to The LORD of HOSTS!!

All scripture references are taken from the King James Version of the Bible, unless otherwise noted.

Introduction

Geneses

Natural Birth Record: October 7, 1943

Spiritual Birth Record: Baptized in the Precious Name of our Lord and Savior, Jesus Christ: January 1, 1967

Baptism of the Holy Spirit: January 4, 1967 (Approx. 3:45 PM)

The Dedication
March 27, 2013

A very sorrowful incident occurred in my life yesterday…my beloved sister, Genevieve Pamela Springer, (affectionately known as *Gen*), passed away unexpectedly. Unbeknownst to us, she was suffering from a life-threatening disorder, and though no one is sure as to how long she endured it, I truly believe in my heart, that had the family been made aware of her suffering, critical advice could have been shared with her—possibly allowing us to have her with us a while longer. Nevertheless, the Lord knows… essentially, to many of us, she was "*a picture of good health.*"

Thinking back, I remember when Gen was born. I was a very mature 6-year-old (soon to be 7), assisting my mother in every way possible, from changing diapers, to bottle-feeding, grocery shopping, babysitting, and the like. As time progressed, I began to feel and assume the role of "Lil Mother". Gen was a pleasant baby and such a joy to care for! I'll never forget how proud my father was when she was born. He named her Genevieve Pamela—PĂ-MELA (puh-MELLA), not (PAM-e-le).

To my parents were born seven girls and four boys. Mother gave birth to six girls in a row, then four boys (the last two were twins), and finally the youngest, my baby sister, Rosalie. Carol and Shirley are the two eldest, I am the third, followed by Marion, Bernice, and then Genevieve. All six of us were born at home, while each of my younger siblings, Willard, Douglas, Curtis & Cecil (the twins), and Rosalie, were all born in the hospital.

I fondly recall the great care and concern I had for Gen. Well, not just for her, but also for all of my siblings, respectively. However, out of them all, none provided me with quite the spiritual testimony as she did! Well into her adult years, she proved to be a great asset to her family, friends, saints, and co-workers. Thank God, she was saved and sanctified. I miss her dearly already! Although she was baptized in Jesus' name in 1967, she had not solidified her spiritual walk with God until February of 1976.

Now, it must have been approximately two or three months after my becoming saved that my husband and I first invited her to church. Many years later, once I knew she was in the process of seeking God for the baptism of the Holy Spirit, with every opportunity, without hesitation, and with all faithfulness, I would make special trips by her home to pick her up for church. All the while, I was about eight months pregnant, expecting my ninth child, Rodrick W. Stevenson (whom I will write about later in this book). Nevertheless, on one particular Sunday morning, I called Gen as I normally would, but she didn't answer her phone. After calling several times more, to no avail, I proceeded to church with my husband.

At some point during morning worship service, one of the deacons informed me that I had a telephone call. All that morning I had been worrying and wondering why I had not heard from her. Naturally, I exited the sanctuary, headed towards the phone booth and picked up the handset; but, before I could even say *hello*, the caller on the other end was already speaking. I was startled and completely taken aback once I fully recognized that someone was in the midst of rejoicing and speaking in tongues! Almost immediately, I thought, "*That sounds like Genevieve!*" I began to call her name and she answered, "*Yes…,*" intermittent with tongues! Instead of rejoicing with her, I was filled with indignation.

I was enraged and anxiously found myself asking, more so demanding, to know her whereabouts. Sternly, I asked, "*Girl, where are you?!!*" When she divulged the name of another organizational ministry I didn't agree with at the time, I LOST IT… TOTALLY LOST IT! That news delivered a sharp pain that generated at the base of my tailbone and quickly shot up the path of my spine. My heart hurt as though I had been impaled – like I had been pierced through with an arrow! Rocked by the news, with tears flowing down my face, I literally dropped the handset, cradled my belly, and just wept. I was wondering if I would make it out of that little phone booth with my mind intact!

Subsequently, I uttered words that weren't very pretty, and before I knew it, I said, "*That ain't nothing but the de…!*" Notwithstanding, before I could get the last syllable of that ugly word out of my mouth, it was as though the Spirit of God, Himself, had prevented me from verbalizing it! For a few seconds, I stood dazed and quieted within myself, introspectively thinking and saying, "*My Lord, I almost blasphemed! The devil doesn't bestow upon us the Holy Spirit! Lord, you are NOT the author of confusion. You are in full control and make no mistakes! Oh Lord, please forgive me!*" Needless to say, I finished talking with my sister and she explained to me that the Lord directed her that morning as to where she would go, and that she was to get there by way of public transportation. She continued to share how the missionary workers called all those seeking God to come down to the altar, and how, without "tarrying", the Power of the Holy Spirit just fell on her!

At that moment, and well into the decades that followed, I began to seek God with much diligence because I knew something wasn't adding up—something was missing relative to my understanding! His Word admonishes us to, "*…let God be true and every man a liar*" (Romans 3:4) and, "*if any man hate his brother, he is a murderer*" (1 John 3:15)! I realized I had been taught only in part. The Lord is gracious, merciful and true. The Apostle James affirms that "*if any man lacks wisdom, let him ask of God, for He gives to all men liberally and upbraids not*" (James 1:5).

From that phone booth experience in 1976, came a great awakening for me in 1979. The Lord called me into the ministry with a three-part dream (which I will discuss later in this book). The dream, coupled with the experience I had in the phone booth, led me on an extensive search throughout the Word of God—from Genesis to Revelation. In the process of time, through much fasting and prayer, the Father has graciously REVEALED unto me many GREAT truths in His Word, which He has also impressed upon me to share with his people. Praise His Holy Name, forever! GOD WANTS NO DIVISION AMONG HIS PEOPLE!

Childhood Memories

I recall very little about my childhood before age 5— other than wearing a red plaid dress with a big white collar, and my mom walking me to school on the first day of kindergarten. However, ages 7 and 8 were quite exciting and recreationally rewarding! Growing up, we longed for the outdoors—my parents allowed us to play outside almost all day. My favorite games were hide-and-seek and hopscotch, and riding my bike and engaging in different facets of jumping rope also proved to be very gratifying. We could play freely and didn't seem to have a care in the world, but playing in the mud was vehemently forbidden!

Sometimes, as the sun settled and all of the day's activities ended, I found myself gazing into the night sky, observing airplanes pass overhead, or following the sequential movement of various searchlights as they rotated back and forth. I often reminisce about the many times I just sat marveling and wondering at the bright stars that so beautifully illuminated the endless sky. Everything about the heavens seemed to shine with such radiance and glory. Even at such a young age, these things caused me to wonder about God.

Although those times were filled with joy and pleasure, my childhood years also came with many responsibilities. My mom would often send me to the grocery store alone, but I thoroughly enjoyed those solitary trips shopping for her. I was so proud of the fact that she had total faith and confidence in my ability to carry out such a task, and at times, thoroughly trusted and depended on me for many other important household duties. As a matter of fact, I can't think of one instance where my behavior even remotely disappointed her. Consequently, she would often reward me with the "leftover change"— all of which I would use to buy treats for the both of us.

I was also quite inquisitive at that age about what most would consider "adult" in nature, although it probably had a lot to do with my Dad taking me to my Uncle George's funeral a few years prior (around age 4 or 5). Of course, before then, I had no concept of death but still found it quite intriguing. I know that may sound a bit unusual for a child, but I was genuinely interested! Sometime before the wake, Dad and I went to visit his widow, my Aunt Lucille. She was rather young and attractive (as far as I can remember), and oh how sad and grief-stricken she was! For some reason, I was the only one of my siblings our Father decided to take to their house, and to the funeral service; to this day, I am still not sure why.

The funeral home was packed! I can still sense the energy that filled the room that day, and can still envision the heaviness and sorrow in everyone's faces. Dad walked me to the front of the room where the casket lay and then extended his hand as he helped me climb up the stepping stool so that I could view my uncle's body. I just stared at him and wondered in amazement. I can't say why, but I was completely in awe of death!

During these same years, each time my mom would send me to the grocery store, I would stop by *Diggs Funeral Home*, which was approximately two short blocks away from our housing complex. I don't think I ever shared this with her, of course. With each visit, I would go in with confidence, fearlessly viewing the bodies admitted there—all of them, from adults on the first floor to the tiny infants on the second floor! I'd go on these secret little excursions, repeatedly, all by myself! Can you imagine doing that at that age? How amazing! The mystery of death raised further questions in my mind concerning the power of God, and even more so, the undeniable reality of His existence.

Moreover, at ages 10 and 11, my level of curiosity concerning the Lord had strengthened, and my pursuit to learn more of Him is even more vivid in my mind today than it was at that time. That year, our family moved into a home where the previous occupants had left boxes of Christmas ornaments and other religious decorations upstairs in a little storage space in the corner. Quite often, I found myself spending hours beholding, examining, and re-arranging the decorations; especially the ones we refer to as the "*Nativity Scene.*" What a true pleasure that was for me!

Those moments brought me such joy and contentment, that when I learned my parents were not financially able to purchase Christmas gifts for us that season, I didn't fret or utter one complaint. Instead, I simply found myself reasoning within and embracing the fact that Christmas was not about the act of giving (or of the receiving of gifts), but that it represented Jesus' birth. The reality of the *"Nativity Scene"* really began to overwhelm my young mind, and before I knew it, this wonderful feeling immediately settled over me. That was such a wonderful experience…in fact, it was so very wonderful, that tears began to flow and all I could do was wish that moment would never end! Unfortunately, for me, it left! That most wonderful feeling faded almost as quickly as it flowed in, and I found myself thinking, *"Just what does this experience mean? Could this feeling have come from God? If only I could experience that sensation once again!"* Not too soon afterwards, we had to move again and leave all of those religious artifacts behind—but that short-lived experience planted a tiny seed that remained hidden in my young heart.

Ages 12 and 13 were very challenging years for me; though, at the same time, they allowed me to establish a deeper spiritual connection with the Lord. This point in my life genuinely brought about a more intimate level of closeness with Him and confirmed the reality of His existence. Unfortunately, that realization would come under very unpleasant circumstances. I say *"unpleasant"* because I had become severely ill, which necessitated God stepping in and intervening on my behalf. On returning home from school one day, I had a very high fever and strep throat, which quickly led to my being unable to walk and fully function on my own. The pain pulsating throughout my body had become so extreme, that my parents would actually have to pick me up to take me to the restroom.

For weeks, my father tried his best to treat me at home, until finally, he decided to call the City Physician. The evening before he called the doctor, as I lay asleep in bed, I suddenly found myself, more precisely, my spirit, mysteriously floating against the ceiling, enabling me to look down at my body while I remained suspended above it! Contemplating the matter, I wondered, *"What am I doing up here?"* Hovering there felt really strange, and smelled of Sulphur. I will never forget that event! The following day, the only other detail I can remember, after the doctor's examination, was the fact that he exclaimed to my father, *"Had you not called me, by the next morning, you would no longer have had a little daughter!"* I believe I had a near-death experience the night before, surely defining how critical my situation was. Consequently, I was admitted to the hospital.

My entire stay there was very lonely and quite painful. Lonely, because my parents couldn't visit me every day, and quite painful, because I was constantly being poked with needles (for one reason or another), the entire time I was there. Not to mention, that once, or sometimes twice each day, without fail, I received hypodermic needle injections full of penicillin (alternating between each hip to alleviate relative swelling) —which was quite agonizing and terribly painful! I was suffering silently, I thought, until one of the nurses saw me crying and asked, *"What's wrong?"* I expressed to her a deep sadness over my desire to go home.

She asked if I believed in God and I said, *"Yes."* *"Well,"* she said, *"Pray! Pray real hard and ask the Lord to let you go home."* I told her that I would, and I did! The Lord heard my cry and answered my prayers, and shortly thereafter, I was discharged and allowed to go home! As a result, my stay in the hospital was only five or six weeks, as opposed to other patients in my ward. There were at least six to eight other individuals there months before I had arrived. A few of them actually cried when the doctor came in unexpectedly, saying, *"Young lady, would you like to go home?"* I was so amazed because my legs were so terribly achy and swollen, that I could not even zip up my boots! My whole body had shed its skin and was still peeling because of the extremely high fever.

Of course, I certainly did not hesitate to say *yes*—no questions asked! Yet, due to the critical nature of my ailment, the doctors explained that I had developed a permanent heart murmur and that I had to limit my physical activity. My father was so protective of me after that, and carefully monitored all of my physical activity. All throughout my remaining years in middle school and senior high, swimming was unconditionally off-limits. My Dad considered it more strenuous than any other activity, even though he had no knowledge of my level of participation in other sporting events at school.

In spite of that particular restriction, I became quite athletic and engaged in many other types of recreation. Riding my bike with "no hands" was one of my favorite outdoor activities. I became so good at it that I could even turn around corners! Kickball, baseball, and running track were also lots of fun, although, later on, basketball became another one of my favorite sports—along with modern dance. I was quite optimistic about majoring in choreography and ballet in college, but that desire faded after I wed and had my first child. I was happily married and genuinely had no regrets.

My high school years were very enjoyable. As a senior, I had greatly improved my academic performance during the final two semesters, received several accolades for scholastic achievement, and finished that year on the honor roll. It felt great knowing I had earned the second-highest overall grade point average amongst the entire graduating class. I was equally proud of the fact that I had also received the highest average in my first-hour Economics class. Though earning the highest mark in first hour was one of the highlights of my senior year, that specific class would soon come to mean something even greater.

I didn't date until after graduating high school—though I never thought that once I decided to do so, it would be with the young man who sat directly behind me in that first-hour Economics class. His name is Mr. Walter Lewis Stevenson, Sr. Before we began our courtship, I was fairly apprehensive about entering into a relationship with him. Even though he was always very cordial and seemed very well mannered, I still had my reservations. First, I exceeded him in age by 10 months. I discovered the age gap when we shared our grades one semester before graduation, and when he let me see his report card, I noticed both his birth date and his address.

Consequently, I was astounded, and even more-so, bothered by the fact that he and his family were living in the very home we moved out of ten years prior to their moving in. While others may perceive that as somewhat providential, I was completely turned off by it. Nevertheless, I never imagined that exactly a year-and-a-half later, on October 2, 1965, I would become Mrs. Jacqueline Stevenson. Ironically, I realize now that '10' is a very significant number in our coming together.

Again, I am 10 months older than he is; he was living in a home our family moved out of 10 years prior to that; and, we were married in the 10th month (which also happens to be in the same month I was born).

After 47 years of marriage (now 52, since the first manuscript of this memoir), 13 pregnancies (12 live births), 16 grandchildren, and 1 great-grandchild, I am still amazed at the fact that we both accomplished so much (12 children), by the prime age of 37! Without a doubt, I give all honor and praise to the Lord for His bountiful blessings!

"To God be the glory for all of the things He has done."

Jacqueline and Walter, Sr. –
Senior Pictures, Southeastern H.S. 1963

Stevenson Family Picture
Walter, Sr.'s Retirement Dinner—2013

Miracles upon Miracles!

Miracle (1) –
Salvation

God truly has done many great, awesome, and miraculous things for my family and me! Of primary and utmost importance is the awesome fact that He saved my soul. The message of the gospel concerning His miraculous virgin birth, sacrificial blood atoning death on the cross, and his victorious, glorious resurrection from the dead, overwhelmed and captivated my heart and soul. I was 23 years of age at this precious time in my life. I was thoroughly broken, contrite, and truly repentant! After being water baptized in the precious name of our Lord and Savior Jesus Christ, I was filled with the gift of the Holy Spirit (just shortly thereafter)!

As I recall, my baptism was on New Year's Day, Sunday, January 01, 1967. On the following Wednesday, January 4, with the presence of God falling upon me, I was filled with the Holy Spirit, accompanied with the evidence of speaking in other tongues (as the Spirit of God gave the utterance). Awesome! Many people were astonished that I fully and willfully inclined to submit myself to the Lord in such a manner. It may have been because I was eight months pregnant at the time. Many of the sisters in the congregation expressed how brave they thought I was, because, ordinarily, women in that condition would not even consider being baptized.

Approximately two months after the birth of my second son, I became extremely ill again. This sickness was extremely painful and much more severe than the first condition I suffered with as an adolescent. At age 12, I was diagnosed with scarlet fever, which is critical enough; but this ailment was a BEAST—it was rheumatic fever! It was so brutal and different from what I had experienced before, that I simply couldn't fathom what it was. Before I decided to go to the hospital, I was bedridden for nearly three weeks. During that time, my father, and especially my two eldest siblings, pressed me to go to the hospital.

I refused because I felt that the Lord would deliver me; but they continued to call me, relentlessly, begging me to go. My eldest sister even threatened that my husband and my pastor would be lying in the grave next to me—if the situation ever became fatal! Her indignation was solely driven by the fact that she felt my leaders were religious fanatics, using me as a guinea pig. What I endured was certainly a testament of my faith and complete trust in the Lord—a level of commitment and devotion they were verily unwilling to accept. However, by God's Grace, I overcame that situation, and my family eventually realized and accepted the fact that my commitment to God was steadfast (and certainly genuine). Praise His Holy Name Forever!

Miracle (2) – In-filling of the Holy Spirit

Have you ever asked yourself what was most important in your life? If so, were you satisfied with your answer? I believe being saved, sanctified, and justified by Jesus Christ and the Spirit of God supersedes any and everything one could ever imagine. For me, New Year's Day, Jan 1, 1967, was a date like no other… everything about that time is still so very vivid in my mind. My husband and I, after having decided we wanted a relationship with the Lord, chose to visit a small church on Chalfonte and Fairfield in Detroit. A few of our family members already belonged to that church and surely welcomed our visitation. However, for me, it became much more than a mere visit, because I know for sure that I had already made up in my mind that I would be *"saved"*.

Consequently, after the message went forth, the time came for alter-call. The conviction to answer the invitation weighed heavily upon me, and because I was so very broken and contrite of heart, it was utterly impossible for me to remain in my seat and not respond. Even though I was eight months— expecting my second child —I was baptized in the precious name of our Lord Jesus Christ. Many of the members marveled at the fact that I would choose to follow through with baptism (in that condition). They kept acknowledging what a *"brave little thing"* I was! My husband was baptized that day as well. After completing this process, the next step, according to scripture, was to receive the infilling of the Holy Spirit, but we were admonished to wait until the following Wednesday instead.

Naturally, the ceremony for water baptism took place on Sunday, but the three-day delay proved to be a very challenging waiting period for me. I say it was very difficult because once we returned home Sunday afternoon, the anticipation of receiving the Holy Spirit overwhelmed me and I simply could not wait! There was never any doubt in my mind as to whether or not it would happen; I just knew that I was going to receive the gift! Nevertheless, the pastor made plans to drive us to the home of a very seasoned and dedicated couple in Pontiac, MI, and instructed us to fast from midnight Tuesday until 4:00 pm that Wednesday. Monday came, and I awoke with an even more heightened sense of joyfulness and anticipation.

That afternoon, I had gone down to the basement to wash clothes, and all that was on my mind was receiving God's Gift. As I meditated upon His promise, I began to weep. I could feel (what I believed to be) the presence of God upon me so strong until I could not continue with my chores. I recall putting the clothing aside and felt led to go upstairs. Once there, I proceeded to the living room and got down on my knees in front of the armchair. As I felt the Lord's presence getting stronger, I became apprehensive, and unbelievably, I actually softly whispered, *"Lord, I think I'll wait until Wednesday like the pastor said… after all, I don't want to wake up my husband."*

Isn't that something? Has anyone ever heard of such a thing, virtually asking the Lord to wait a while later to bless me with His precious Holy Spirit? What was even more amazing and wonderful was the fact the presence of God, along with the anticipation of receiving the gift, did not wane. It remained so heavily upon me until it was hard for me to "hold it off", so-to-speak, and all I could do was wish for Wednesday to hurry up and come! Subsequently, Wednesday came, and I fasted for nearly 16 hours, just as the pastor requested.

The time finally came for him to drive us to Pontiac. It seemed like the ride there took forever. While my husband and the pastor were engaged in (what I considered), idle chatter, the reward of what was to come was at the center of my thoughts, and the conversation between the two of them seemed so far removed. My expectation of receiving the Holy Spirit was extremely high, and to me, that was all that mattered! If only they would stop talking!

We eventually reached our destination, and as soon as we walked towards the front entrance, Mother Corr greeted us at the door. I remember her sweet smile as she introduced us to Elder Corr. *"Well, we know what we're here for… ladies first,"* she said, pointing the way into her moderately arranged bedroom.

She then offered me a seat in a small chair across from the bed, and we both sat as she began to explain what the scriptures said I should expect to experience. Barely minutes into her presentation, she stopped short of her speech once she noticed me crying and wringing my hands. I truly desired for her to stop talking, and that's exactly what she did. *"Oh, let me stop talking; I can see you are ready!"* With that, she immediately stood up and began spreading newspaper across her mattress and onto the floor. Beyond my teary-eyed, and now somewhat blurred vision, I was a tad perplexed as I observed her movements. I sat quietly wondering what her reasons were for doing so.

Nevertheless, her actions were not enough to deter me in the least bit. I went there knowing I would receive the Holy Spirit, which was all that mattered. Mother Corr instructed me to kneel at her bedside and then directed me to repeat the words, *"Blessed Jesus"*! She began repeating, *"Blessed Jesus,"* in a very fast-paced cadence (as if she wanted me to follow her lead), but by that time, I could not even talk! The tears were rolling down my cheeks and I attempted to utter the phrase, but the only thing I was able to say was "ble… Jee…" before my tongue became rigid and began to move in a circular motion. My arms flew up in praise to God and I began to speak with other tongues as the Spirit of God gave the utterance.

The most astounding detail about this experience was that I had no prior knowledge about tarrying, or about speaking in tongues. My encounter with the Spirit of the Lord was fresh, genuine, and authentic. I had never witnessed anyone praising God this way; there was nothing I had to refer to, and there was no way for me to mimic anyone else. I'm sure my unborn son Tracy, who is now an ordained Elder and Pastor, must have felt God's power too (because of the way he moved around inside of my womb). After a while, Sister Corr finally said, *"It's been at least 45 minutes since you started."* Then I heard her remark that I sounded like a little bird. Praise God for the blood. God is faithful and sure to deliver on His Word without man's help! Thank the Lord for His Unspeakable Gift. GLORY TO HIS GREAT NAME!

"Who can find a virtuous woman? For her price is far above rubies"
(Proverbs 31:10)
My Spiritual Birthdate: January 04, 1967

Miracle (3) – Beyond Conception

The Lord would often give me the unction to fast and consecrate myself before Him. His Holy Spirit was my constant companion during times of prayer and intercession. Together, they have proven to be my hiding place and shelter from the tests & trials, and tribulations of life. In the heat of spiritual warfare, they are actually two of the most powerful weapons necessary for us to defeat the enemy! The Word declares that, "*The weapons of our warfare are not carnal, but are mighty through God, to the pulling down of strongholds*" (2 Corinthians 10:4). With that, I humbly share how the Lord intervened in a mighty way… again!

After my bout with rheumatic fever, doctors warned me not to have any more children. They also surmised that I would have to receive a monthly dose of penicillin shots for the next five years—but I refused their advice. This warning came only after my second child. Did I not claim to have had 13 pregnancies, and 12 live births? My God is a wonder! My first-born son is a licensed, ordained elder with pastoral experience, and my second eldest son is currently a licensed, ordained elder and pastor. All of my other children, in varying degrees, are God-fearing men and women, and so are all of my grandchildren. Praise God!

Miracle (4) –
Beyond the Shadow of Doubt

When I initially began having children, I delivered four beautiful healthy sons in a row. Unfortunately, during the birth of my fourth son, the attending nurse attempted to prevent him from being born before we reached the delivery room. When he was nearly a month old, we discovered that her reckless maneuver caused him to sustain a specific type of neck injury, which I had no knowledge of—at least at that time. Whatever she did affected the muscle in his neck, causing his head to twist to one side. It was so tightly constricted and drawn in until there was no way I could even wash in between his neck while bathing him. Of course, I became deeply troubled about his condition and knew that I had to seek the Lord for an answer.

During prayer, I would plead and ask the Lord to reveal to me what was wrong with my baby's neck. Eventually, He turned my attention to a newspaper article describing his condition to a 'T'! The article explained that hindering an infant's birth will, or can cause a condition known as a wry neck. Apparently, the injury affects the neck muscles, wherein they become constricted, causing the head to twist to one side. The injured muscle continues to tighten on one side and can only be surgically corrected by cutting the compressed area to relieve the tension. "*Oh, Jesus!*" I thought. "Lord, *you know I cannot stand the thought of those doctors cutting on my baby*", I cried! I felt led to go on a three-day fast to further seek God's help. That was my ONLY hope!

On the third and final day of the fast, the Lord led me to pray and lay hands on my son, but I let either fear or reluctance overtake me. I'm not sure which one it was—although, in the end, the results are synonymous. Nevertheless, I felt defeated and full of remorse for not following through with God's directive. Close to another month had elapsed as I watched the condition worsen.

Consequently, the impression to repeat the process weighed even heavier upon me, and I could not possibly resist! I began the second fast, totally abstaining from food and water for three straight days. On the third day, anticipation was high—I mean, exceptionally high! At the appointed time, I picked up my baby, took him into my bedroom and sat him on the bed. With both hands clasped firmly around his little waist, I went down on my knees, and as I was descending, I began to feel the very presence of the Lord showering down upon us. His presence was so heavy until I immediately began to weep and bury my face into the mattress. I could not hold my head up! The last thing I saw before I fell into that position was my baby boy's head tilted and fixed to one side, almost touching his shoulder.

Nevertheless, praise be unto the Most High! After the anointing of God ascended, I was finally able to lift up my head, and through teary eyes, I saw that my baby boy's head had straightened up and was positioned normally, just as it should be! HALLELUJAH! GLORY TO GOD IN THE HIGHEST!! My son's name is Lawrence Anthony Stevenson, now the father of three beautiful girls and a worshiper whom God has delivered mightily! In addition to this mighty miracle, the Lord has brought him victoriously through many other dangers, toils, and snares. He owns a successful small construction business and is prospering in the favor of God—Praise His Holy Name, forever!

Miracle (5) –
By the Word of Faith

Another condition befell me one day that eventually had me bedridden, hardly able to swallow, and unable to eat. Initially, the symptoms were mild. I had a sore throat, accompanied by a slight fever, but soon, the condition became excruciatingly painful and nearly unbearable. Naturally, I had no idea what was wrong, so after a few days of suffering, I began to seek God for direction. I had inquired of the Lord several times but had not yet received an answer. It wasn't until the next morning, as I lay on my back, feeling the warmth of the brightness of the sun against my face, I asked God one last time, saying, *"Lord, what is wrong with me?"* As soon as I had asked the question, it seemed like a type of ticker tape, or computer readout, composed a thought in my mind, which simply said …*"INFECTED TONSIL."*

Suddenly, my strength was restored from within, seemingly out of nowhere. I remember getting straightway out of bed and dressing relatively quickly because I felt led to go to the hospital for an examination. When I arrived, the attending nurse asked a number of general questions, and then sent in a doctor to examine me. He asked what my symptoms were, and what I thought could be wrong, and I told him, *"I have an infected tonsil."* He looked at me and firmly asked, *"How do you know? Have you ever had this problem before?"* I said, *"No, I haven't."* He then replied, *"How would you know that?"* and I confidently replied… *"God told me!"*

Boy, the look…I tell you if one could have seen the expression on his face, especially after he examined me and found it was exactly as my Lord had informed me! God is just awesome… and then some! The doctor simply wrote me a prescription for antibiotics and quickly exited the room. Well, the blessing didn't end there. After I took the prescribed antibiotics, the infection cleared up and all was well for a while. However, some months later, the same affliction fell upon me a second time.

Subsequently, I didn't allow nearly as much time go by as I had before, and I had no desire to go back to the hospital. As a matter of fact, I began to talk to the Lord and said, *"Lord, I don't feel like going back to that hospital! What if I were stranded on an island somewhere, unable to access doctors or medication? I have the power of Your Holy Spirit and I don't feel I should have to depend on mere man, when your power is sufficient*! Right then, the Lord directed me to go down in prayer—to SPEAK to that condition and COMMAND it to leave in JESUS' Mighty Name! I obeyed immediately, speaking to that condition in Jesus' name, as instructed. By the Almighty Power of God, the condition left instantly! Glory, Hallelujah! Isn't God a wonder?

"Many are the afflictions of the righteous, but the Lord delivereth [them] out of them all" (Psalm 34:19).

Miracle (6) –
Rain Down Healing on Us

As I pen this experience, I am presently visiting with my youngest son, Rodrick Wesley Stevenson (affectionately known as *Rod*), in Rosenberg, Texas. He and his lovely wife of four years, Elizabeth Lijin, have a two-and-a-half-month-old baby daughter, Isabelle Charlese—who's as beautiful as can be! Adjusting to parenthood—while having to adjust to job changes and a new environment— became a bit overwhelming for them. Subsequently, they expressed how desperately they needed my assistance; so, here I am.

During his teenage years, Rod was and still is a very avid and accomplished basketball player. Likewise, during those years, he was a street and pulpit minister of the Gospel. He has traveled the world, played with stars of renowned, and has acquired several college degrees. Before he left home, he would spend just about all day either playing ball, or sometimes, spend half the night witnessing. Either way, whenever he retired for the evening, he would be so worn-out, that he would just lie down and go to sleep with his shoes on. Well, it's a known fact that gym shoes can generate terribly unpleasant conditions if not used properly.

Consequently, a very serious and unpleasant condition developed on his feet that started between some of his toes. Initially, we were able to treat all of the infected areas, except for one crucial spot. He had developed a foot fungus that spread to the top of one of his feet, and no matter what measures we took to remedy the condition, it continued to worsen. We consulted countless medical professionals, but to no avail. The last doctor we conferred with told us that he would prescribe the strongest medication they had for his condition and that there was nothing further they could do. Even though the top layer of the skin appeared to heal, the fungus continued to worsen, progressively breaking down the deeper layers of tissue beneath the skin.

I worried as I observed the immense swelling on his foot, noticing that the infection began bloating from the inside out. It had gotten so bad, that he wasn't even able to wear shoes. Well, this particular day, I remember calling him downstairs for something, but can't recall why. What I do recollect was the horrible sight of his foot when it landed on the bottom stair. It was so severely swollen that it shook like gelatin! The fungus had burrowed deeper into his foot, causing it to become severely infected, raw, and runny on the top. When I saw his condition, all I could do was call on Jesus! I fell on my knees – there was no fear or apprehension of laying my hands on that frightful looking sight.

I was completely overwhelmed and fully focused as I felt the heavy presence and anointing of God overshadowing us. Just as before, when the Lord so graciously healed my son Lawrence's neck, He manifested His great power again! With my head buried in my chest, I just wept and waited for the anointing of God to leave. His presence was so strong until I couldn't lift my head even if I wanted to. When the Lord finished, I removed my hands and observed that his foot had instantly been healed! Every ounce of the swelling was gone, and there was only a very small grayish layer of scar tissue in place of the raw and runny infected skin! We are both yet overwhelmed to this very day. This miracle has truly been an undeniable mainstay in my son's life. Truly… To God be the Glory! ALL OF IT!

Miracle (7) –
My Miracle Baby

At the age of 37, I delivered my 13th child, my youngest daughter, Francine Regina. Because she represents a life and death situation, and much physical suffering, I call her my little pearl of great price. During the second to last month of my final trimester, I began to experience premature labor pains, and my water broke. My dear husband rushed me to the hospital only to learn that I could not deliver the baby right away. After several ultrasounds, the doctors diagnosed me with a condition known as *placenta previa*. This meant that the baby could only be delivered by Caesarean, as the placenta lies very low within the uterus, covering the birth canal.

Well, that seemed rather common, but what was uncommon, or even more exceptional, was the fact that the placenta was not only blocking the birth canal, it was attached to the major blood vessel leading to my heart, which was located in the lower back part of my womb. From a medical professional's perspective, it was something that hardly ever happened! As a result, they informed me that six pints of blood were on reserve especially for me. They repeatedly asked for my consent to administer it, but I had no intentions of relenting or compromising. I had a hard time refusing their many offers, until finally; I tried to implement a little levity into the situation. I jokingly remarked that since they let me know the blood would be from some 26-year-old male, I would not want it because it might make me grow a mustache! That didn't work either. To them, this was certainly no laughing matter!

I expressed, in no uncertain terms, my faith and trust in God, and that only He could preserve and sustain me. They observed my bible, which I would read and keep open on my nightstand, but they never gave up. Finally, the head physician came to me alone one morning and said,

"Jacqueline, you are such a lovely young lady. I would hate for something to happen to you, where you would have to leave all of your beautiful children and your husband behind. When it comes time for us to deliver the baby and the afterbirth detaches from your major blood vessel…it will literally rip it wide open. Just like you turn on a faucet full force, that's how your blood will be lost, and you will bleed so fast and go into shock before we will even have a chance to give you a transfusion. Please, just for our peace of mind… won't you please sign for the blood?" I replied, *"I'm sorry, my decision is still no."* "Well," he said, while glancing at me, then at my bible, then back at me… *"Jacqueline, the only way you can survive this situation is IF God intervenes!"* I replied emphatically, *"That's exactly what I'm expecting Him to do!"* He could only sadly walk away.

I was in the hospital about a month before the scheduled delivery date of March 16. I was very miserable and uncomfortable because I could not lie down the entire time I was there. Since the placenta lay below the baby, it shifted her position upwards, pressing her against my lungs and heart. I had to remain in an upright position because it had become quite difficult for me to breathe. Not being able to lie down meant they could not examine me nor administer any type of lower body anesthesia. Their only recourse was to inject the anesthesia into my arm, directly into my bloodstream, then hurry through the delivery before the anesthesia could reach my baby. Surely, for her, that would have been fatal!

Now comes time for the Caeserian delivery….

Now a few weeks before the surgery, the doctor who initially examined me and diagnosed my condition refused to continue to treat me because I had rejected his advice. But, to my surprise, and to my dismay, instead of the warm-hearted doctor who sat at my bedside, this other doctor would be the one assigned to actually perform the surgery. He began his incision just below the navel and began to rip downward. With the sinister look on his face, even behind his protective mask, I could see that he was being very vindictive, as he knew the anesthesia hadn't sat in, and that I was obviously still awake! Only the Good Lord knows the nerve throbbing, excruciating head and back pain that I experienced. It felt like my head was being thrashed back and forth after that wicked doctor plunged his sharp scalpel into my swollen, tight stomach.

Just before I passed out…I could hear myself let out a loud blood-curdling scream— something perhaps like one might hear in a torture chamber! After the delivery, the time came to remove the staples from my incision. The head physician that came to me prior to the delivery, stopped in to see me once again, but this time, his mannerism was much different. He did something that I had never known a physician to do. He actually came and sat next to me on my bed! He looked me square in the eyes and said, *"You know, Jacqueline…that which we said would happen- did happen! But, the bleeding stopped,* (snapping his finger emphatically one time) *it cut off, just like that!"* he exclaimed. Then, he just sat there for a few more minutes looking at me – then at my bible, and then back at me. I cannot, word-for-word, remember all that we discussed. After our exchange, he then stood up, wished me the best, shook his head while shaking my hand, and simply walked away. He was truly overwhelmed… I'm sure!

Francine is now a thriving adult and a great joy to our hearts. Still today, I choose to call her my miracle baby, my little pearl of great price. God knew that I would often declare that this was an experience (that I often felt in my heart), was something I never wanted to go through. Actually, it went far beyond that! He allowed my greatest fear to come upon me, and as a result, I adopted the scripture from the book of Job 13:15- "*Though he slay me, yet will I trust him.*" GOD IS A WONDER. HE IS A WONDER IN MY SOUL AND A VERY PRESENT HELP IN THE TIME OF TROUBLE! THANK YOU JESUS! THANK YOU!

My miracle baby and Me on her Senior Prom
May-1999

Miracle (8) – Restoration of Life

Sometime during her late teens, my miracle baby, Francine, had become extremely ill. Her symptoms equaled that of about five different afflictions! She had a fever so high, she said her brain felt like it was on fire. Her eyes were very sore and red, and it was hard for her to focus. Moreover, she was very, very weak, and her body ached to the point that she was totally unable to stand, or walk. She was very congested, with thick reddish-brown phlegm that had a strangely infectious odor. I discerned that what she had was contagious, so I would not spend much time in her room when I went in to care for her. I would constantly ask her if she wanted to go to the hospital, but she repeatedly declined. Yet again, my pearl of great price would be the object of God's miracle-working power.

Around 10:00 PM that night, I was very tired and wanted to go lie down. I went back to her room to check on her again and asked if she wanted to go to the hospital. She very faintly replied no. I became even more concerned, feeling a greater urge to encourage her to go. I asked, *"Sweetie is something else wrong?"* She faintly whispered, *"I… can't breathe…"*

"Jesus!" was my first and only response, and before I could even think, I felt myself automatically going down on my knees and finally lying prostrate over her. The power of God rained down so heavily upon us; I could not even speak, but could only intercede silently in the spirit. I don't remember anointing her with oil or recall whether or not I had any at all. That prayer must have lasted at least 15-20 minutes. After God's anointing left… I stood up and proclaimed healing, in Jesus' Name. I said, *"Sweetheart, I believe God has touched you. I'm very tired, so I'm going to lie down and come back later to check on you."*

Well, after nearly two hours, I returned to check on my baby but found her still lying in the same position she was in after the prayer… I asked, *"How do you feel?"* She replied, *"I can't feel anything!"* Alarmed, I asked, *"you can't feel anything?!!"* Thinking she meant she was paralyzed or numb, but quite the contrary! What she meant was that she no longer felt any pain, discomfort, fever, congestion or anything else related to her condition. One can only imagine the joy and thankfulness I felt after that, knowing that God had undoubtedly healed her (completely), of every symptom! She immediately stood up and began to smile and flex her body. Needless to say, we offered thanksgiving and praise to our God and gave Him the Glory as we rejoiced in His Holy Name! What a Mighty, Mighty, MIGHTY God we serve!

Miracle (9) –
Irene's Deliverance:
(When the Doctors say, "No")

Irene is a former co-worker and good friend of my eldest daughter, Marlena, the fifth oldest child amongst her siblings. My daughter called me one day, quite concerned and upset because Irene had become terminally ill and said that the doctors had given up on her. She had been diagnosed with an incurable form of pneumonia. Naturally, I grew equally alarmed and concerned and began to pray and intercede on Irene's behalf. Rochelle, my second oldest daughter, similarly showed concern, and being led by the Lord, the two of us agreed to fast and pray for God's intervention.

After fasting for three days, Rochelle and I headed straight for the hospital, up to ICU, and into Irene's room. The atmosphere was quiet and still, and the room was very dimly lit. Irene was slumped lifelessly on a very low portable cot, and sitting next to her was a machine with a big round container on the floor, half-filled with what appeared to be a dark red or purple-looking fluid. We soon realized the machine was extracting it from her lungs! Her head was slanted to one side and her skin was ashen and dry. When I laid eyes on her, I could only begin to softly, and repeatedly, call on Jesus. Rochelle also began to call on the Lord. Then, I began to talk to Irene. At first, it seemed as though she did not hear me. We tried to get her to respond, and gently encouraged her, too, to call on Jesus.

The nurses kept entering in and out of the room, checking her vitals and adjusting the IV. Although we knew their attending to her was hospital protocol, it was a bit distracting. Consequently, my daughter locked the door and stood guard while I spoke to Irene. I tenderly told her to say *"Thank You Jesus… Thank You Jesus… Thank You Jesus…"* She could only pant half breaths… then merely pant again. I reached for the small vial of oil I usually kept in my purse but saw that it was empty. My daughter said, *"Mom, all we need is just one drop. Let's turn the bottle over and let it run down until we get enough on your fingertip…"*

I was in total agreement, waited for that one drop, and then anointed her forehead with oil. We both laid hands on her and began to pray! The nurses frantically tried to gain access to her room, but my daughter refused to unlock the door. God began to move! After we finished praying in Jesus' precious name, we continued admonishing her to say *"Thank You Jesus."* As soon as she uttered those words of praise, she slowly began to hold her head up and speak half words, then whole words. Her natural skin tone returned and she began speaking fluently, saying *"Thank You Jesus! Thank You Jesus!"*

When my daughter opened the door, there were approximately five nurses and a head doctor standing outside the room. They were noticeably unnerved, but once they came in, they were totally astounded and perplexed at how alert and coherent she was! She was breathing normally and the fluid appeared to stop draining from her lungs. After careful observation, they unhooked her from the machine, and immediately afterwards, she walked over to her large bed, climbed into it, and even stood on top of it and started jumping up and down! Appearing quite perplexed, one of the physicians asked, *"What happened?"* The staff was also noticeably confounded and continued to probe for an explanation. Irene exclaimed, *"It's those Sanctified Prayers! It's those Sanctified Prayers!"* Immediately, we corrected her, letting her know, clearly, and in no uncertain terms, the glory belonged to the Lord.

Glory, Hallelujah! Other nurses began entering the room to witness her dramatic and miraculous turn-a-round. Among others were my daughter Marlena, her husband, and Irene's boyfriend. All three of them were equally astounded, but her boyfriend didn't know what to think! He looked at us and asked, *"What did you do?"* Undoubtedly, he was well aware of Irene's critical, near-fatal state, and knew the doctors emphasized that she was not going to make it. I took him aside and began to explain to him about the Grace, Love, Mercy, and Healing Power of God! He had so many questions—the kind of questions that indicated to me that he was one who would not be easily convinced.

Finally, when the conversation ended, we noticed that Irene was busy entertaining her other visitors while casually eating my son-in-law's curly chips. When we arrived, she was on a feeding tube, and by the time we left, she was consuming solid food. Our God is awesome; bless His Holy Name forever!

Approximately two years later, my husband and I saw Irene at the grocery store. When she saw us, she charged towards us yelling, "*Mommy, Mommy so good to see you! How are you both doing?*" We exchanged pleasantries, talked intimately about what had caused her illness, and relished in the miracle the Lord had so graciously performed in her life! Even though Marlena does not have a personal, critical, or life-threatening experience of her own to share, I thank the Lord for Her God-given wisdom and faith in His miraculous healing power. Without His Spirit, she would never have been mindful enough of the sense of urgency to request intercessory prayer for her friend. Had she not been spiritually connected, this testimony would not exist! Thank God from Whom ALL blessings flow!

Miracle (10) – God's Undeniable Handiwork

My second oldest daughter, Rochelle Lanette, whom, as I said, accompanied me when we went to minister to Irene, has been a truly faithful and dependable daughter. She has been my right hand, in helping with household chores, from cooking, to babysitting, to home improvement projects—you name it! She reminds me of the dutifulness and support I devoted to my mother as a child. I often depended on her for many things and she never disappointed me. I recall a particular incident when she was approximately 13 years of age, where she almost became an amputee.

She and her younger siblings were playing in the house and she somehow cut her finger on the edge of the mirror connected to her bedroom dresser. My husband was home at the time, but I was at church. By the time I returned, Rochelle and my eldest daughter were standing in the bathroom with her hand immersed in a sink full of bloody water. My husband had rushed out to buy a number of first-aid products to attend to the wound. It bled for quite some time until we were able to stop the flow and wrap her finger with cotton balls and medicated gauze strips.

In fact, the cut was to the bone of her ring finger, only we didn't know the extent of her injury at the time. Unfortunately, we made the mistake of attempting to treat it ourselves instead of seeking proper medical attention. Nevertheless, we allowed the bandage to remain on too long and the cotton material had become enclosed in between the tissue of her finger as it healed. Her hand was swollen, and she said she felt a strong tingling sensation as we unraveled the band. In order to remove the cotton material, we had to rip it away from her finger, which re-opened the wound, causing it to bleed. Moreover, we detected that it had lost its normal color, and had developed a very foul odor.

I felt that if I soaked it in disinfectant, this would help resolve any possible infection (so it seemed). The following morning, while she was at school, she complained of having a dull throbbing tingling sensation in her left hand, all the way up to her elbow. Well, her gym teacher asked to see her hand and was alarmed at the appearance of the open wound. She called home and admonished us to seek immediate medical attention; after which, my husband and I decided that we should take her to Children's Hospital. After being thoroughly examined by a host of doctors, they expressed to us that Rochelle had no feeling in her hand, that the infection had reached her bone, that her finger was dead, and that the contamination was spreading to the rest of her fingers, and up her entire arm. They were contemplating amputation because her finger had turned dark grey, indicating, as they had determined, that things had progressed too far.

They admitted her and immediately administered IV to counteract the infection. I prayed with her before going home and continued seeking the Lord about it all night. Naturally, when I discussed their diagnosis and intent to amputate her finger, and possibly more, with my husband, he was vehemently against it. I called Rochelle the following day and told her to pinch her hand to see if she could detect feeling, which she confirmed she did. She also told me that her finger was itching and that she had feeling in the palm of her hand. While we were on the phone, one of the attending nurses came in to deliver her breakfast and saw my daughter scratching the wound. Naturally, the nurse was a bit shocked to see that her finger was itching and asked what was wrong.

Rochelle complained that it had been bothering her all morning and that she had feeling in the affected areas. The nurse hurried to get the doctor, who rushed in with a team of specialists and began testing for life in her hand. One of the first signs they noticed was that its normal color had returned–the swelling had gone down, and that she again had feeling. She also exclaimed that one of the doctors was squeezing her hand so hard until his hand actually started shaking! They then began to poke at it with a variety of sharp instruments and were amazed that she had natural feeling in it, and that the wound was healing without stitches. They kept her on IV for another week-and-a-half, and then released her from the hospital, minus the need of any further treatment.

To this day, her finger bears only a very thin scar (as a reminder of the wonderful healing power of the Lord). Praise God, from whom all blessings flow… for He is a God who never fails!

Miracle (11) – Confirmation in a Dream

A few years later, Rochelle developed a condition, which by description, strongly suggested pneumonia. She complained of constantly coughing up bloody phlegm, her chest, ribs, and side hurt, and she had no desire to get out of bed. I decided to go up to her room to anoint her with oil and pray. What's so amazing is that before I went to anoint her, she said she dreamt that I was walking up the stairs with a bottle of oil, and then stood over her, laid my hands on her chest, and began to pray. That's exactly the sequence of events that took place, and right before I reached down to touch her, she immediately awoke and called out my name.

The dream took place, simultaneously, while I walked up the stairs towards her room. I still anointed her with oil, laid my hands on her, and prayed. One hour later, she emerged with a victorious report of healing, and that all of the pain, soreness, the inability to breathe, and all of the constant coughing and bloody phlegm had ceased! Is there ANYTHING too hard for our God? Bless His Holy Name! Believe and you shall receive!

Miracle (12) –
"No Good Thing Will He Withhold…"

Many times, or should I say, most times, when the Lord would give me the unction to fast, I would have some understanding as to why. This particular time, I was simply being obedient to the voice of the Lord. I distinctly remember the impression coming on a Tuesday, the second day of a consecutive three-day fast. Of course, total abstinence was my usual practice, with nothing to eat, and nothing to drink. Many times, I would often do so while expecting children. Nevertheless, this particular Tuesday, I was standing in my kitchen, leaning against the cabinet connected to the sink, meditating on the goodness of the Lord.

At that moment, He proclaimed in my spirit, *"You ALREADY have the victory!"* Amazed, I questioned in my heart, *"Lord, over what? The fast isn't over until tomorrow!"* The revelation of that impression did not immediately occur to me, and even though the Lord spoke those very affirming words in my spirit, the thought of prematurely ending the fast never entered my mind. At the appointed time, I ended the fast that Wednesday, as planned. The following day, I was downstairs in the basement, and my daughter, Rochelle, was there with me helping with some spring-cleaning (as she so faithfully did).

Speaking of the basement, as I recall, the Friday evening prior to my having started the fast, my husband and I were downstairs having a discussion. He was sitting at the desk in a small room that we had converted into an office, and I was standing next to him. In the midst of our conversation, I received a very strong impression about asking him to make a minor adjustment to the basement window. A few years prior to this, for security purposes, he had permanently sealed its wooden frame to the concrete base of the wall by driving a 4-6 inch nail through it. After asking him to remove it, I said, prophetically, *"…yeah sweetheart, you just never know."*

Well, knowing my dear husband, I expected him to say *"no"*, but to my surprise, with no questions asked, and without rebuttal... he simply asked, *"Where's the hammer?"* Happy, yet amazed, I scurried to get it and watched as he pried that nail away from its concrete base with the type of ease and finesse that only a 6-foot-plus man could! Immediately after removing the nail, we carried on with our discussion as though we were never interrupted. As a matter of fact, I think spring cleaning was part of the discussion, which, again, is why Rochelle and I were downstairs that following Thursday. I was standing by the washer not too far from the stairway, and she was standing right at the foot of the stairs. For some reason, I told her to take a load of trash outside and empty it. She said, *"But Mom, it's not even full enough yet."*

Nevertheless, I demanded that she take it out right then. As soon as she left out the door, one of my sons, who was helping his Dad refill one of his recreational vehicles, hurriedly opened the same door and sat a gas can on the landing. In haste, he let the door slam, not realizing that the can had fallen over and toppled down the stairs. Within seconds, it hit the concrete floor and exploded. Flames immediately engulfed the stairway and nearby surroundings, shot backwards toward the furnace, and then upwards across the basement ceiling towards me. Plumes of thick, toxic, jet-black smoke completely filled the whole area. It was so thick, that I could hardly see anything, nor could I even manage to take one breath! But, God!

I sit crying as I write these words, unable to fully process the miraculous sequence of events—knowing I was trapped in the fire. What a Mighty God... Hallelujah! He instantly brought to my mind the nail that my husband removed from that window just six days prior to that. Also, had he not removed the nail, I could never have told this story! That was my only escape! Furthermore, had I not sent Rochelle out with the trash, by her standing right next to the stairs, in even more imminent danger than I was; she would have instantly been engulfed in the flames! Oh, but I'm so glad that the Lord proclaimed two days before, that, *"[I] ALREADY [had] the victory!"* What a Mighty God we serve! I observed my family all running frantically towards the back of the house, headed for the basement door as I was climbing out of that side window. God only knows the horror and fear in their hearts and the thankfulness in mine.

We later saw how the flames had traveled up into the kitchen and completely gutted it. The fire would have engulfed the dining room and the rest of the entire house as well, but we know the Lord must have said, "*Not so.*" I say this assuredly because the dining room is directly adjacent to the kitchen, and the curtains in that room were completely burned and had fallen away from the rods onto the carpet, but not even one of its fibers was singed. Moreover, nothing else in the home was affected, nor was there any smoke damage beyond that point! The fire just stopped! The following day, I stood again, leaning against the cabinet—fully observing the charred ruins in my kitchen—thanking God for sparing our lives (and the remainder of my home). Almost instantaneously, the presence of the Lord came upon me, and ascending from my belly, I could feel the power of God rising… flowing like a river into a sustained cry. It reminded me of the scripture that says, "*…out of your belly shall flow rivers of living water*" (John 7:38).

I had later found this emotional expression to be described as a "SHABACH"— *a loud, sustained cry, a praise unto God by His Spirit.* This occurred on Friday. Two days later was Mother's Day. Customarily, I would stop by my mom's and fellowship with her and my other siblings. In the midst of relaying my experience to them, especially when I expressed the part where the Lord told me, "*You ALREADY have the victory,*" my sister Genevieve, (whom I've just lost), gasped and exclaimed, "*Jackie, my pastor just preached that message this morning! The title was, 'You've Got to Know that You Already Have the Victory!*" God is truly a wonder and He always confirms His Word! He's just Good, Great and Greatly to be Praised! He is truly a Mighty, Mighty Deliverer!

THE DREAM

Dreaming is such a phenomenal function of sleep. While some dreams are hardly worth remembering, others are relatively more profound and well beyond any natural desire of readily forgetting. Likewise, I believe God inspires exceptional dreams of this nature, prophetically. One such dream that I would like to share, which happened several decades ago in 1979, I trust, came directly from the Lord. One night, in the month of March of that year, the Lord gave me a three-part dream. Likewise, by which, He called me into the ministry. The dream began with my stepping inside the entrance of my church, only to find that it was flooded and in pitch-black darkness.

Being able to proceed no further, I heard the voices of some brothers, and there seemed to be much commotion going on. The next thing I remember was that someone had removed a license plate out of the drain (which allowed the water to recede), and handed it to me, after which, I accepted it and left out of the building. As I walked away, the plate, which appeared to be made of pure gold, became more illuminated by the extreme brightness of the sun, revealing the inscription, *'BLACKSMITH BLACK-SMITH BLACKSMITH'*, in beautiful fancy black letters. I proceeded in the direction of the parking lot, closely examining the plate I held in my hand. At that moment, the scene changed to my standing on the bottom stairway of an escalator, going upward. On the other side of the escalator, which was moving in the opposite direction, I saw a brother who was, at that time, Chairman of our Young People's Department.

As he continued towards the bottom of the escalator, I reached over, handed him the license plate, and proceeded to go up the ramp. When I reached the top, the scene changed again, this time, to my entering into a small upper room, which appeared to be something out of ancient history. It looked as though thick dust and cobwebs had accumulated everywhere, even on the floor. Directly in front of me (to my left), I saw a very narrow doorway.

After making my way over to the opening, I realized it had no door, and found that, instead, it was a small crude closet. I looked inside and saw a huge pile of old-fashioned ancient looking men's shoes of different styles and sizes, also laden with layers of dust and cobwebs. I picked one of the shoes from the pile, which was almost reaching the ceiling, looked curiously at it, and then slowly sat down in the middle of the floor.

With the shoe in hand, I asked the Lord in my heart, "*WHAT MEANETH THIS?*" It was at this point I immediately woke up. I was never so overwhelmed in my life! Each time I relay this dream to someone else, I would always get chill bumps. Needless to say, I began to search the words: *blacksmith, water, darkness, shoes,* and other facets of the dream and found them all to have very deep spiritual connotations. Upon discussing this dream with my Pastor, five years later in 1984, he immediately instructed me to start attending Minister and Teachers' Meetings, for he felt the dream to be God-inspired and that the church needed to make some ministerial adjustments.

He forewarned that he felt (or realized), those changes wouldn't be made overnight. In actuality, this dream is the foundation of a paper God inspired me to write in 1998, concerning brotherly love continuing and the obliteration of strife, hatred, and controversy over the Godhead. This dream of 1979, coupled with the experience I shared earlier in this book (i.e., my sister receiving the Holy Spirit in 1976, at another institutional church instead of receiving it at my assembly), led me to seek God for more wisdom and understanding concerning Him. Eventually, I began an extensive study of His Word, from Genesis to Revelation, while He, Himself, revealed the many hidden truths within the text—hidden mysteries which pertain to Him. To this end, nearly 34 years later, the church did suffer a disastrous flood. This, at this time, is when I believe that some members (a select few), began to gain a better understanding of the true Deity of Christ.

HALLELUJAH!

The Paper:
(ca. December 2, 1998)

The following is a copy of the paper the Lord led me to write. It reads as thus:

"BLESSED ARE THE PEACEMAKERS":
(FOR THEIRS IS THE KINGDOM OF GOD)

PRAISE THE LORD BRETHREN:

It is time and due-time for God's people "<u>EVERYWHERE</u>" to be at peace with one another letting brotherly love continue… with love unfeigned.

Organizationalism, denominationalism, and pursuits for positions, titles, power, and material gain have greatly <u>wounded</u> the body of Christ, and have also resulted in numerous <u>splits</u> and <u>divisions</u>. This is said to be the <u>ultimate</u> in <u>carnality</u>.

For the past 23 of the 32 years I have been saved–I have carried the burden of reconciliation for the people of God, torn apart viciously, by traditions and issues concerning the Godhead.

(Being led of the Lord):
Through much prayer, supplication, fasting, grief and concern for God's people, I have come to this point in time to go forth and accomplish God's call in my life.

(Being led of the Lord):
For <u>years</u>, I have prayed for the opportunity to be in the midst of a host of leadership

to share these very important issues. God impressed in my spirit that the welfare of the people, and all that must be accomplished, begins with leadership. Mutual reasoning is a <u>must</u>!

(Being led of the Lord):
To fast, pray, and extensively study His Word concerning the Godhead, and being <u>called</u> to teach and share what I have learned of and from <u>Him</u>. Over the years, I have sought answers from <u>man</u> unsuccessfully, but <u>God is faithful</u>. I am therefore asking that you would be so gracious as to yield some of your time— as I have matters of <u>great</u> <u>importance</u> to discuss; which are vital to us <u>all</u>. So much <u>time</u> has already been <u>lost</u>.

It is my hope that we all may come to a better understanding of one another, as it is God's Divine will that we be able to comprehend with all saints. (I have consulted with my pastor on this past Sunday, and I am hereby requesting to speak with you, <u>as a group,</u> in Jesus' name).

I am looking forward to a meeting <u>soon</u>. Please contact me as soon as possible.

God bless you and thank you!

Humbly,

Evang. Jacqueline Stevenson

THE SAVIOR'S DATE OF BIRTH

Another paper the Lord moved upon me to research and write is one concerning the true birth date of our Lord and Savior, Jesus Christ. The year was approximately 1998, our Sunday school lesson, at that time, stemmed from the Book of St. Luke 1:2

THE 6TH MONTH - PRAISE YE THE LORD
Please read entirely, St. Luke Chapter 1

St. Luke 1:26
"And in the sixth month, the angel Gabriel was sent by God unto a city of Galilee, named Nazareth..."

St. Luke 1:27
"...to a virgin espoused to a man whose name was Joseph, of the house of David, to a virgin named Mary."

SYNCHRONIZED JEWISH CALENDAR

NOS.	NAMES OF MONTH	FARM SEASONS
1 (7)	NISAN (Mar-Apr)	Begin Barley Harvest
2 (8)	IYYAR (Mar-Apr)	Begin Harvest
3 (9)	SIVAN (Mar-Apr)	Wheat Harvest
4 (10)	TAAMUZ (Mar-Apr)	
5 (11)	AB (Mar-Apr)	Grape-Fig-Olive Ripe
6 (12)	**ELUL (Mar-Apr)	Vintage Begins
7 (1)	TISHRI (Mar-Apr)	Early Rains - Plowing
8 (2)	HESHVAN (Mar-Apr)	Wheat – Barley Sowing

9 (3)	KISLEV (Mar-Apr)	Begin Barley Harvest
10 (4)	TEBETH (Mar-Apr)	Rainy Winter Months**
11 (5)	SHEBAT (Mar-Apr)	New Years for Trees
12 (6)	ADAR (Mar-Apr)	Almonds Blooming
13	ADAR SHEIN (Mar-Apr)	Intercalary Month

Month of Conception (ELUL): Elul is the 6th month, and it means "TO SHOUT FOR JOY"

AT VINTAGE. Vintage means harvest, particular year of period of origin, also Excellence-Maturity.

Read *PSALM 100 and *PSALM 8

*Counting down 9 months from ELUL You will find the month of Sivan.

Month of birth Sivan: Sivan is the 3rd Month and it means "Appoint" or "To Mark".

Take special note of God's timing — Wheat Harvest!

TO APPOINT: means to name to fill an office or position. Jesus was given a name above every name... also, read Luke 19:10, 22:29, 22:69.

TO MARK: a recognized standard of quality... to notice... pay attention to. To serve as a guide, to single out; a visible sign or symbol. Read Psalms 37:37 (Mark the perfect man and behold the upright...).

Everything God does has meaning and purpose. Even these months chosen by God for Jesus' conception and birth- as you can see are very deeply typical and spiritual. God, as you well know, more often than not, uses the natural to signify the spiritual! AWESOME!

HARVEST: A time when "First Fruits" of the crops were offered to God. (There were 3 harvest times each year- Barley, Wheat, Tree and Fruit of the Vines).

FIRST FRUITS: offering unto God the first ripened fruit of the crop. From a spiritual standpoint, we are to present our bodies (an offering unto God) a living sacrifice Holy and *acceptable (remember Cain?) unto God. Read Romans 12:1. Our fruit is righteousness of the spirit – by the love – grace and mercy of God. Read Galatians 5:22 and Ephesians 5:9 *Also, Jesus is the first fruits of them that slept… I Corinthians 15:20-23 *The First born from the dead. Colossians 1:15-18

WHEAT: 7 ears in one stalk. 60-100 grains per head, which were roasted over fire. (Referred to as "parched corn") Leviticus 23:14, Ruth 2:4, I Samuel 17:17 and 25:18. **Read: Matthew 13th chapter, regarding the parable of the Wheat and Tares. *Please note that grains (30-60-100) per head are considered "fruit brought forth"

BARLEY: Bread – staple food, (grains) of Hebrews. A symbol of poverty and scorn

PASSOVER: Season of Barley Harvest. (Exodus 23:16)

FEAST OF PENTECOST: 7 weeks later – When Harvest. (Exodus 34:22)

FEAST OF TABERNACLES: 7th month fruit harvest…

Jesus was not born on December 25. He was not even born during the winter months. According to St. Luke 1:26 "And in the "sixth month" the Angel Gabriel was sent from God unto a city of Galilee, named Nazareth… (unto Mary), prior to this glorious event – Elizabeth (her cousin) had also conceived a son in her old age and was at the time, also in her sixth month; but had hid herself for 5 months.

*Jesus was and is – The "Hidden" Invisible, Wisdom and Eternal Power and Godhead. (Read Romans 1-20) His time of supernatural conception, by the Holy Ghost overshadowing Mary, is "Hidden" by Elizabeth's 5th and 6th month experience.

God's word does not pinpoint the day of Jesus birth – neither are we instructed to "celebrate" it. What we are carefully instructed to do both by Jesus and by his apostles, is to commemorate His death through Communion. (We show forth his death till He comes.) Also note that celebrating one's birthday or birthday parties, are not supported by scripture and was not originally a Christian practice – nor was it practiced by the first church. Pagan practices of "honoring one on his date of birth" every year, should never be compared to the worship Christ received through gifts (at age two with his mother in a house). This was a one-time event, not a lifetime event.

Praise the Lord! (An Update)
The 6th Month…The 3rd Month…The 6th Day

As it was stated formerly, and now a further study regarding the true birth month of our Lord and Savior Jesus Christ, has resulted in these interesting and overwhelming facts.

According to Saint Luke 1:26, the Angel Gabriel was sent to Mary in the 6th month. According to the Jewish Calendar, the 6th month was Elul. This was the month Mary conceived. Nine months later, she gave birth to Jesus in the month of Sivan.

- Elul is equivalent to our September – October.
- Sivan is the equivalent to our May-June.

Through study has found that Jesus' birth month, Sivan, is (for centuries), the exact same month Pentecost was celebrated, every year on the 6th day.

Please consider these important facts and similitude:

1) Pentecost: Celebration of Wheat Harvest. Wheat is a grain of the earth – 7 ears in stalk with 60-100 grains per head (roasted over fire is <u>parched corn</u>) Grains bringing forth fruit 30-60-100 per head. Wheat is to be harvested with a <u>first fruits offering</u> of crops to God.

*The saints are the <u>wheat</u> (not tares of the earth)… precious grain – to bring forth <u>fruits</u> of <u>righteousness</u>. Some 30… some 60… some 100-fold. Our offering is our bodies – A <u>living</u> sacrifice. We are the harvest to be gathered.

2) <u>Pentecost</u>: The church was born on Pentecost Day. <u>Why?</u> The church is the <u>Body</u> of our Lord and Savior Jesus Christ. He is the <u>Head</u>. If this is the birth date of the <u>Body</u>, it is also (for them to be one) the birth date of the <u>Head</u>. Hence, (I believe) Jesus was born in the month of <u>Sivan</u>, on the 6th day. (June 6th) For centuries, that was a natural type and shadow of the spiritual birth of Christ and his body, and all things pertaining to character.

*Everything pertaining to Pentecost (a) wheat, (b) harvest/increase, (c) first fruit offerings, etc. pertains to the church!

Also, note: The <u>Harvest</u> of <u>Increase</u> of Jesus. (He's the ear corn, which had to die and went into the ground/earth)

*He's parched corn (tried by fire or fiery trials)
<u>Jesus' Increase?</u> Jesus brought forth from the 12 disciples 120 souls on the Day of Pentecost (10 x 12) Also 3,000 + 120 all in one day… Hallelujah! What an increase!

Does the number <u>10</u> (possibly an offering) have any significance? (Possible 10% tithe?) Representation? What is your opinion? (Smiles)

Christ and his body (The Church) is by its descriptions, attributes, and character, the <u>ultimate fulfillment of Old Testament "Pentecost."</u>

Love and Prayers…

God Bless You,

Evang. Jackie Stevenson

Miracles upon Miracles
(Part 2)

Miracle (13) – An Elder's Deliverance

It was what seemed to be a usual Sunday morning. We were busy preparing for church. We had seven children to dress (all "stair-step" - from ages 7 to approx. 4 or 5 months), and plenty of necessities to pack away in the diaper bag, sufficient for every need. Usually, around 8:00 A.M. or so, my husband would leave en-route to pick up the East Side church members who were in need of transportation. He faithfully served as a driver for the ministry for roughly two or three years. Before leaving, his usual manner was to remind me that he would stop back by the house to get the children and me and for us to *"please be ready"*! He wanted to ensure everyone arrived on time for the Sunday School lesson.

Up to that point, everything was ordinary; but as soon as I bid him farewell, told him to be careful, closed the door and turned to resume my routine…the presence of the Lord came upon me. With His anointing came a foreboding impression and a fear over the loss of life. Almost instantaneously, He told me to begin fasting! *"Yes, Lord!"* I replied. Fighting through tears, I asked the Lord, petitioning to know the details. Again, I asked, *"Lord, who is it? Will my husband have an accident while driving the church bus? Lord, who is it?"* He gave me no answer, but I immediately started fasting without delay. Whatever I had planned to do that day didn't matter, for the Lord had spoken.

At the appointed time, my husband returned for us, having incurred no problems at all, and although I was naturally very happy and thankful, my heart was still heavy because of the impression I received prior to his safe return. The remainder of that day went as usual, and though fasting was not what I had planned for the day, being faithful, steadfast, and obedient to the leading of the Lord took precedence over everything else. Monday found me yet fasting and looking to the Lord, but still no answer. Around 4:00 in the afternoon, the telephone rang; my sister in law was on the other end, both excited and devastated as she informed me that our 2nd Assistant Pastor had been shot in the head during a botched robbery attempt in the church's pastoral office. The Lord confirmed within me—that was my answer!

That same evening was designated for Young People's Service, which I attended. Although I was still fasting, I said nothing about it, or the prophetic utterance, to anyone! By God's grace, I continued fasting until Friday. This was the first and only time that I fasted consecutively for five days straight. After breaking the fast that Friday evening, I also attended Saint's meeting. Coincidentally, after service began, one of the presiding elders announced that the church would be going on a three day fast for that situation, starting midnight Sunday. Would you believe that I fully participated in that fast too? The power of God is just amazing!

It's a blessing to know that I can do all things through Christ, which strengthens me. I am still amazed that the Lord led me to start fasting and interceding one day ahead of that tragic incident! We all praised God for his mighty deliverance, thanking Him because it could have been fatal. God granted him 39 more years of life—in spite of that horrific attack. Bless God's wonderful name forever!

Miracle (14) –
The Surgery

My eldest son, Walter Jr., invited me to be his guest for an evening event on the Detroit Princess; a pleasant Gospel Cruise on the Detroit River, sponsored by friends he knew from church. The food and fellowship were enjoyable, and I had eaten to my heart's content. We were mindful of the time that we should leave because we had to prepare for church the following Sunday morning, so we were careful to return at a reasonable hour. The next morning, I found myself not feeling well at all, but knowing how I felt about missing service, I still pressed my way to church; especially because I had to teach Sunday School.

Midway through the lesson, I began to feel increasingly ill, so much so, until my husband and I eventually had to leave church. During the drive home, the pain grew increasingly worse, and even more intense as the day progressed. By evening, and all throughout the night, the pain intensified in some areas of my body more-so than others. The next morning, I decided that if things didn't change, I would go to the hospital and have the condition examined. I remember thinking, *"Lord, I've prayed for so many others, but now, I find it hard to pray for myself."* The pain made it too difficult for me to focus; I simply couldn't concentrate.

By mid-day Monday, I decided to go to the hospital, and my dear husband was more than willing to accommodate me. No sooner than I had arrived and gotten my vitals checked…all of my children had begun to gather there as well. When the doctors expressed to them my need to have surgery, immediately, things became very chaotic! They explained that the initial step would be to remove any gastrointestinal fluids and that they would have to insert a tube into my stomach through my nostrils in order to extract all of the bile from my stomach. We all felt that the procedure was a bit much, but to our surprise, it was relatively quick and painless. I signed off on the consent forms, and the technician inserted the tube within less than two-three minutes.

After being admitted and assigned a room, the attending physician explained the type of surgery I would need and scheduled a time for the operation. In the meantime, I had no idea that many of my other relatives had filled the hospital chapel, and that my youngest son, Rodrick, and his wife, Elizabeth, even flew in from Florida. My pastor and his wife made a brief visit and excitedly exclaimed that I didn't even look ill! *"Look at her skin and her hair! Are you sure you're ill? Well, probably not, she's just sick and tired of us…"* I was so amazed to hear their kind sentiments but genuinely glad and thankful unto the Lord they came to visit me. As far as I can remember, a few days passed before my scheduled surgery—during which time, as I mentioned earlier— things had become slightly chaotic. From this point on, I will let my eldest son, Walter Jr., finish detailing this experience (because there were a number of other important details I did not have the privilege to witness).

Thus… According to my Son….

Walter's Testimony:
(*A Miracle from the Lord!*)

After having received a call from my brother, who, by the way, begins by saying, "*I've gotten an update on Mom's condition…*" (this, he says as if I had already known she was sick), I rushed down the highway from out of state. I drove eight straight hours and arrived at the hospital, exhausted from the journey, only to witness my mother in a hospital bed connected to a machine with a host of tubes and wires. She had been admitted with complaints of excruciating pains in her stomach and abdomen. The doctors had taken her off solids and liquids, and after the three days of totally abstaining from food and drink, in addition to many tests and x-rays, the team of doctors and surgeons concluded that there must be a blockage in her intestines—which ultimately prevented her from being able to digest or eliminate food.

Without digestion of food, minus the ability to eliminate waste, I knew that she would scarcely survive. The situation had become dire and time was not on our side, because the longer she went without eating or drinking, or even receiving supplemental nutrients intravenously, the weaker her body became. Around the fourth day, the surgeons began to warn that unless they were able to perform a critically necessary gastrointestinal procedure, they would not be able to locate the obstruction. We realized that without having any other way to determine or pinpoint where the obstruction was, the doctors were completely in the dark, and Mom's situation would become more critical.

The strategy they deemed necessary was a "best-case scenario." The procedure involved their making an incision, which would start at the bottom of her breastbone, then down into the abdomen, just below her navel. They would then have to remove her entire stomach and intestinal cavity, feel throughout her large and small intestines (in an effort to find the obstruction), repair the affected area, and then finally restore everything so that she could successfully regain normal functionality of her digestive and elimination processes. The surgeons stated that the operation was so serious that she might not survive either the operation, or the recovery.

They also acknowledged that there was a slight risk that they may not find the source of the blockage, or that there could be life-threatening post-surgery complications. Because of the weakened state she had fallen into due to the mandatory four-day fast, the situation had quickly evolved into a matter of life or death. Nevertheless, the team scheduled the surgery, in spite of (the now) five consecutive days with absolutely no food or drink, or any other form of nourishment to aid in preserving her strength during the operation.

As always, my mother seemed to have complete resolve in her faith in God. She and I had been the only two to hear the doctors' discussions regarding the details of the surgery; since my father and other siblings were not at the hospital when those conversations took place. At that time, Mom told the doctors that she had put total control of her health and well-being, and any decisions regarding her hospital care, into my hands (at the leading of the Lord). The burden of that decision weighed heavily upon me, so I felt compelled to go on a fast.

I knew I had to seek the Lord for wisdom on how to manage hospital visitation schedules with family, friends, and loved ones who wanted to see her, as well as receive direction regarding hospital care, administration of nutritional supplements, pain medications, and other treatments the doctors and nurses prescribed for her during recovery. The other serious factor that manifested was the threat of dangerously high blood pressure, which spiked several times, threatening stroke or heart failure. In all of my life, I had never been more frightened and stressed about anything like this before. We needed God to work a miracle!! Our backs truly seemed to be up against the wall!

The Lord began to show me what to do, initially instructing me on how to establish order for everything regarding my mother's care (before and after the surgery). The first directive was to organize a team of intercessors and implement a prayer regimen pertaining to her situation. I went to my church, at that time, and met with the lead missionary and the primary prayer warriors and explained the gravity of the situation so they could fully ascertain what God had instructed me to do. I shared that I was fasting and also needed some of them to stand in agreement with me, as this was, by far, the most serious situation that I had ever encountered.

Next, was my plan to appeal to the Ministry of Music. As I stood before nearly one hundred choir members during rehearsal that day, asking for their prayers for my mother, I remember becoming very emotional and breaking down into tears. In the nearly twenty years that I had been affiliated with that ministry, I had never once requested prayer for anything. They could sense my level of brokenness and knew that my situation was grave. I could tell what they had discerned by the way that they rallied behind me as they began to pray. It was during this prayer that the Lord augmented my strength and increasingly began to undergird me and give me a sense that we were going to get the victory!

Immediately afterward, I began to move with great resolve. I organized a family meeting at the hospital to disclose the particulars of the situation to my father, all of my eleven siblings, some of their children, his closest sister (my late Aunt Barbara), my mother's closest sister (my late Aunt Genevieve), and a few of our closest cousins. The entire Family Room was filled beyond (permissible) capacity as I explained to them what the Lord had told me regarding maintaining order, prayer and visitation protocol, and even that their conversations surrounding the entire process be exclusively full of faith and victory. We held hands, prayed the "prayer of agreement" and then dismissed.

The next morning, my father and I met with my mom, prayed with her, and spoke words of encouragement in the affirmative. I held on to her personal items as the nursing attendants rolled her down to the anesthesiologist. The surgeons had informed us that their projection on the length of the surgery was between 6-8 hours. Once in the pre-surgery area, my father and I prayed once more with her. Immediately afterwards, she said, *"My trust is in the Lord, and I'm in the His Hands*!" We told her that two of her other sons and two of her daughters were in the Family Room, waiting in support. I was strengthened and in awe of her powerful and unwavering resolve. I held her hand and told the head surgeon to take extra care of her. He said that he would personally come back to speak with us after the surgery was over to give details about his findings.

While in the waiting area of the surgery ward, we were diligent in our efforts to focus on conversations that were positive and affirmative. After about 20 minutes, the Head Surgeon came into the waiting room. Of course, all of us initially looked at each other with gripping fear and bulging eyes, wondering why he was standing there so soon with his gloves off. However, after joyfully announcing that the surgery was over and that it was a miraculous success, a chorus of exhales filled the room— along with a unified sigh of relief— as he proceeded to describe what his findings were.

He explained that as soon as he had made the initial incision and began to lift her intestinal cavity, he immediately saw that a portion of her large intestine had slipped in behind a two-inch fissure that had somehow developed there, and that this was the cause of the obstruction. He said that he was able to quickly sew up the fissure and restore her intestinal cavity without any disturbance! He also bragged about how remarkably smooth, healthy, and beautiful her intestines were. He finally proclaimed that it was truly a miraculous event! Lastly, after explaining to us that they had stapled her incision, they immediately took her to the recovery ward.

He also cautioned that the first 12-24 hours were the most critical during her recovery. All the while, I was thanking God for what He had done in the operating room, and now I was praying and putting my trust in Him to give her strength to get through the recuperation process. Two days had passed since the surgery, and I hadn't had a chance to shower or sleep in my own bed because I had spent the night there all that time. The hospital staff was very accommodating – allowing me to have a blanket, pillow, and food during my stay.

Thankfully, Rochelle was able to provide some relief, working in tandem with me while alternating overnight stays; monitoring and supervising her visitation schedule; documenting her milestones and necessary stages of progression; her meal times; medication logs; all hospital staff protocol; and most of all, assisting me with overseeing the total comfort and well-being of our mother.

Over the first twelve hours of the night after the surgery, I sat by my mother's bedside and prayed over her body as she winced in agony and pain while she slept. I remember getting up every few minutes and standing over her to make sure that she was breathing, and I would place my hand over her body and say, "*In the Name of Jesus, breathe [Momma], breathe*!" I declared this repeatedly throughout the night. When she awoke the next morning, I was there by her side. I shared with her everything that had happened after she went to the pre-surgery room. She was weak, but she still thanked God for bringing her through. God had indeed worked a miracle!

Even though her blood pressure spiked dangerously high over the course of a few days, the Lord regulated it without the use of the medication the doctors insisted on her taking. Praise God for my little sister, Erica, for nursing Mom back to health while she recuperated for four weeks at her home! Because of her innate gift of caring for those in need of rehabilitative and private nursing assistance, Mom's progress was quick and steady, and there were absolutely no complications. She had followup visits and eventually increased her food intake to solids with no apparent digestive issues! To God be the glory for the things He has done!

Another Birthday Cake for Mom!

Family Time at Dinner

Miracle (15) –
My Hubby's Dilemma

My daughter Jacquelyn, who is my namesake and 7th child—and who is very proud of it—along with my daughters Melanie, Erica, and Lisa, all relish the fact that the suffering they encountered during many of their childhood diseases was greatly lessened through prayer. Praise the Good Lord; plus, Walter Jr., and Alan Raynard, my third eldest son, both suffered severe cuts from falls as toddlers, and in each case, the Lord miraculously stopped the bleeding. The doctors even remarked in each case that under ordinary circumstances, the bleeding should certainly have continued! Thank God…

As I mentioned before, prayer is such a blessing and an essential, effective spiritual tool. The scripture declares that *"the effectual, fervent prayer of the righteous avails much!"* Sometimes, the essence of a much-needed prayer can actually be consummated when fervently calling on the Name of the Lord! I remember an instance where while I was in the kitchen finishing up on a few tasks, my husband was eating dinner in the other room. I heard him choking and gasping, and as I looked around, I saw him coming towards the kitchen from the dining room. I ran over to meet him, and by this time, he was just inside the kitchen doorway. I grabbed on to him crying, *"Jesus, Jesus,"* as he appeared to stop breathing and fell back against the kitchen wall. Then, his body slid downward with his eyes out of focus. His head dropped, and as his mouth hung open, drooling down one side of his chin. I remember clutching my husband with all of my strength—with all of my might! There was no way that I could hold him up or even think of administering the Heimlich maneuver.

All that I could frantically do, with my eyes closed at that point, was to call on the very God of Heaven, again, repeatedly crying, *"Jesus!"* In an instant,

Praise the Lord... He stopped sliding down the wall – his eyes refocused – he stood up and instantly regained his composure. He seemed perplexed and noticeably shaken, then quickly said..." *I'm alright Jackie, I'm alright...,*" almost as though my alarm was not warranted. He walked to the bathroom and ejected the items that caused the blockage. Apparently, a few large pieces of meat had gotten lodged deep into his esophagus. Don't tell me that my God isn't Great! He truly is a <u>very present help</u> in the time of trouble! PRAISE HIS HOLY NAME FOREVER!

Me and Walt Sr. outside of church

The Dream of March 1979 Revealed to my Pastor in 1984

I praise God for Bishop's insight and his Godly wisdom, in response to my relating this awesome dream to him. Almost immediately after calling him to request an appointment to share important details pertaining to the ministry, he agreed and met with me on the pulpit in the main sanctuary. Before the meeting began, I was under the impression we were all alone, but to my dismay, after I had nearly finished speaking, I heard indistinct sounds coming from behind the curtain in front of the baptismal pool. I immediately suspected that someone stood eavesdropping behind the veil. I tried not to focus on the distraction and continued explaining the dream.

During the course of our conversation, I explained that the Lord gave me the vision in 1979; however, our meeting took place in 1984. He seemed shocked and asked why I had waited nearly five years to share it with someone in leadership. I expressed to him that since I knew it was of a prophetic nature, I was waiting on the leading of the Lord before disclosing any portion of it. I also felt led to wait until the first stage of the dream came to pass...which it did. Consequently, he expressed that he felt my actions and course of reasoning were inspired by God, confirming everything that I had shared with him. *"Daughter,"* he said, assuredly, *"There certainly are some changes that NEED TO BE MADE HERE, but very principally, won't happen overnight! Nevertheless, we will get started. I want you to start attending the meetings for young ministers and teachers."* Even with the confidence I felt he had in me, I knew implementing a new agenda for the ministry would not be easy!

Almost immediately following the meeting, as I proceeded towards the exit—though I had barely made it halfway down the hallway—this brother hemmed me up against the wall, with his finger pointed in my face, and angrily declared, *"You ain't no prophetess, and you ain't gon' do NOTHING in this church!*" I was so shocked and appalled that I almost didn't know what to say! To this very day, I still cannot recall what I said in response. However, I do still remember the level of fear that gripped my heart, and quite naturally, I had considered him to be a thorn in the flesh from that moment onward.

Furthermore, every time the two of us were in the presence of anyone who was younger, it always seemed as though he would become overly antagonistic, or try to embarrass me. My prayer is that he confesses and repents before it's everlasting too late! Regardless of this and other foolish occurrences, I remain steadfast and immoveable. I know God is in full control, and He alone is the head of my life! Truly God's Grace is sufficient in any and every situation!

My First Ministerial Assignment
"Proclaim and Declare"

As I previously mentioned, I was called into the ministry in 1979 by an inspired three-part dream. In 1984, per my pastor's request, I began attending the meetings for ministers and teachers—both of which were very rich and spiritually edifying. However, that same year, a few months after speaking with the pastor, the LORD gave me a very "Serious Assignment." It was a very "serious assignment" indeed!

One afternoon, while praying and meditating over certain unfavorable circumstances—that had for some time existed in the church—in addition to other spiritual matters, I began to lament and seek God for direction and intervention. The Lord then spoke these words to my heart... "*Tell Bishop _____ to repent!*" At this point, I was kneeling at my bedside. I had no immediate desire to follow that directive, and began reasoning with the Lord, asking, "*Lord, ME? Why?*" This simply cannot be happening! By this time, I remember lying semi-prostrate with my forehead touching the floor, crying and reasoning with the Lord. It was as though I could not stand to my feet until I had submitted to the Lord's will concerning the matter.

I cannot accurately recall the amount of time I spent on my face, but I do know that I finally conceded and committed to doing the Lord's will. Soon after my concession, I remember asking, "*Lord, how? What shall I say, what shall I do? Should I write him a letter? Should I take this brother aside privately and tell him? Just what should I do? How should I tell him?*" The Lord simply and plainly said this, "**Proclaim and Declare**." That's all I was given... just those three words. I repeated them several times to myself in amazement—before I came to the realization that, contextually, I had no clearly defined understanding of what those words meant!

I consulted a dictionary and performed a word search, and to my dismay, '***proclaim***' meant: *to cry out; to announce officially and publicly declare; to indicate unmistakably* – while, '***declare***' meant: *to make clear; to state formally or officially; to state authoritatively or emphatically; affirm.* I was devastated! How could I possibly go through with this? The bottom line was, contrary to my deep level of apprehension, the only conclusion that I could solidly embrace in my heart, was, in fact, that the Word of God admonishes us to fear and obey God rather than man. Therein lay my faith – therein was my hope! I knew the Lord would not direct me to do anything without giving me the strength to perform it.

Feeling strengthened and uplifted, I shared this experience with my husband and one of my sisters-in-law. My husband was a bit apprehensive – but she cautioned, "*OBEY GOD,*" which I fully intended to do. The time soon came for our annual convention. Usually, during this week-long course of events, the leadership team scheduled specific times for all ministers to meet in the chapel for spiritual instruction, teaching, and fellowship. Two weeks had already passed since receiving the directive, and I knew from within that my obedience to God would have to manifest at that time.

The first day of the meeting started, and I was mindful to take a seat in the front row. My sister-in-law sat right beside me. The intended recipient of the message just happened to be the facilitator of the instructional portion of the meeting. I'll never forget the topic, "*Know Your Calling.*" How appropriate...for I surely knew mine! The only thing that troubled me, outside of my extreme nervousness, was the fact that the theme of the message did not present an opportunity for me to say anything. I looked at my sister-in-law and exclaimed... "*He's teaching but I need the Lord to open a door of opportunity.*" I think she said, "*He will,*" or something to that effect.

No sooner said than done; that door swung wide open! Simultaneously, she and I glanced at each other (in total agreement), and then she nudged me with her elbow. In a soft, reaffirming tone, she said, "*Alright!*" Well, before I knew it, I stood up from my seat with my knees trembling like never before! He said... "*Yes?*" And I firmly replied, "*The Lord said you have need to repent!*" The room was instantly in an uproar! A few ministers came and pulled me aside and asked, "*What's going on, what did he do?*" He immediately called the meeting back to order and redirected the focus back on to me. "*SHH! Hush,*" he demanded. "*Let's see what she knows.*" As the shock value momentarily faded, I gathered my thoughts, though still quite relatively nervous, I shared with him a few of the issues God revealed to me.

While I was speaking, our soon-to-be Assistant Pastor was sitting directly on the other side of me. The words that I spoke caused him to slide down in his seat, almost slumping into a fetal position, with his hands up covering his ears. He replied in part with what I had to say, but the speaker simply carried on with the meeting. Afterwards, I advised him at least two separate times, because the Lord, again, had said, "*Warn him to repent.*" The last time I approached him, I also apologized, letting him know that it was not I, but the Lord – also reassuring him that he had always been one of my most admired ministers. This was certainly not a personal indictment against him, yet, he merely responded by saying, "*Well, I know you mean well…,*" and we left it at that—so I thought!

From that moment onward, I noticed the attitudes of many had changed towards me. Whenever he was invited back to the ministry to preach, he would make it a point to indirectly attack me as a form of retaliation for what the Lord had given me concerning him. For instance, at times, when I'd either be running behind schedule and enter the sanctuary after the service began or whenever he would spot me already sitting in the midst of the saints, he would immediately change the content of his message.

Once, he started remarking about, "*How tired [he was] of all these little so-called false prophets walking around here!*" He continued on, alleging how their words had him so troubled, he couldn't sleep for six months! Keep in mind; I could hear some of the content of the message just before joining the service, so the abrupt switch was an obvious distraction. He continued on with a mocking tone, again, indirectly addressing me, and declared, "*Psst! Psst! Now, I've got the victory,*" etcetera, etcetera.

I'm a living witness to the sad reality that whenever one takes a stand for the Lord, they incur a loss in popularity and support. Though very painful, I still have my joy and am yet suffering many forms of backlash for my obedience— but praise be unto God! Jesus declares, "*If you suffer with me, you shall reign with me.*" This brother passed away some years later—after much suffering—but there is one thing that I've learned; it doesn't matter what man thinks, no one can exalt him/herself above the Word of God! We cannot love and esteem "manmade" positions (or titles) more than we love and esteem Him! From what I've heard, the Lord was gracious and merciful enough to have sent another minister his way with the same warning. Did he ever repent before the Lord? I don't know. Nevertheless, one thing is for sure, only our Heavenly Father truly does! He is the Just Judge of all the earth, and He will do right!

Miracles (16) – God's Word Confirmed

I believe that the Lord orchestrates certain situations in our lives solely for the purpose of encouraging, strengthening, and increasing the faith of the believer. That which I am about to relate is one such instance (among many). The occurrence is very vivid in my mind, though the specific years are not. A certain elder and his companion, an accomplished evangelist, periodically visited our home church. She would always open with a prelude to her husband's ministerial message with a song of praise. They were both in town to minister for a weeklong revival.

As it is with those who walk with the Lord, I was going through a few tests & trials, and the Lord knew that I was in the right place, at the right time, for some much-needed encouragement. For three consecutive nights, portions of the minister's message would come to my mind the night before. By Thursday night, before the minister even brought forth his message, his words came to me in so much detail, until when I finally heard him speak, I could only sit there in tears. I was so overwhelmed, that I found it very difficult to keep my composure! God truly works in mysterious ways…His wonders to perform! I am constantly in awe regarding his omniscience, omnipotence, and omnipresence! He always confirms his word! *"The name of the Lord is a strong tower, the righteous [run] into it and is safe"* (Proverbs 18:10).

Miracle (17) – Testimony of One Healed

In approximately 2001, the Lord led me to assist in the Prayer Ministry. In more recent years, I have been called upon, periodically, to serve at the altar in praying for the sick, and for those seeking intercession. Some would ask for prayer for general/personal reasons, while others would come forward to accept the Lord. During one of the services, many ministers came forward and availed themselves for prayer because the line was quite long.

At the same time, a young sister came forward for prayer, but they instructed her to come to me. She stood before me with her eyes closed; and after making her requests known, I anointed her with oil and began to pray. In the midst of the prayer, the power of the Most High rained down and overshadowed her. A few weeks later, while the two of us were in the restroom, she began to thank me for praying for her and said *"You know…when I came up for prayer I didn't know which minister prayed for me but I know it was a female because I could smell her perfume. Later on, I saw it was you… You are powerful!"* I said, *"Thank the Lord."*

I praise the Lord for touching her body. Before the prayer, she had lost quite a lot of weight because she had no appetite and wasn't really able to eat very much. Well, not too long after that, I saw her one day in the church parking lot, sitting in her family's car. She appeared to have gained weight, and at that time, was rejoicing while eating a very large lunch. Thank the good Lord for her victory!! Enjoying a healthy sized meal was something she had not been able to do prior to that act of intercession! The Lord is always a very present help in the [time] of trouble! (Psalm 46:1 paraphrased)

Miracle (18) – Delivered…Unexpectedly!

As I previously shared earlier in this book, as a child, I was plagued with two critical illnesses, resulting in my developing a case of arthritis in my joints; but I had no idea what it was until adulthood. I received the diagnosis after suffering from two bouts of rheumatic fever, and one case of scarlet fever. However, sometime between ages 30-35, I went on a three day fast, after which, the Lord graciously revealed to me that I was allergic to eggs and that I should refrain from eating them, along with most dairy products because those things were highly acidic and was triggering the pain in my joints.

At that time, I was suffering from a nagging pain in my left shoulder, and while watching a Christian program on T.V., the Apostolic Minister urged those watching to trust God for healing, which I did. Amazingly, God healed every bit of the pain in my shoulder. I was completely surprised and could not believe it happened for me so quickly. I remember laughing! Instead of thanking the Lord – here I am amazed and laughing shaking my head as if to say, "*I can't believe this!*" Can you imagine?

The following day, I found myself carrying the same attitude. Then I received a phone call; though very brief, one that turned out to be a very serious and engaging counseling session. The caller had revealed to me a very distressing situation, sharing that they had been victimized. I remember telling this individual that the perpetrator shouldn't try to test the Lord. I distinctly recall my words, saying, "*You can't (and don't), play with God,*" affirming to her that the Lord would intervene.

Well…apparently, I was guilty of laughing in disbelief when the Lord touched my shoulder. As soon as the call ended, I was walking towards my kitchen, giving God praise, and about mid-way across the threshold, I felt my footsteps change, as though I was about to rejoice in a dance. Instead, I found myself going down on my knees, with my forehead touching the floor and both arms stretched out behind me. I was in that position for at least five minutes – I could not get up!

All I could do was cry, thanking God and giving him the glory, as he so vividly reminded me of my own words. He had healed my shoulder and I didn't honor him as I should have. I was in awe for the remainder of the day. The next morning, I was even more awestruck when I opened up the day's newspaper and saw a very large picture of a man dressed in Jewish clothing, on his knees – his forehead touching the floor,- with both arms stretched out going backwards! It was the exact same position the Lord had me in and the photo was entitled: "*Gentleman in Ancient Prayer Position in Jerusalem!*"

What an awesome, awesome, experience! Always Give God the Glory and Give Him the Praise… He's Worthy! Worthy! Worthy!

In addition to the revelation, the Lord exposed other foods that triggered inflammation in my body, while the Spirit also led me to vital information that would aid my fourth eldest daughter, Melanie, in managing an asthmatic condition she suffered with since birth. Up until the time of her adolescent years, my husband, her siblings, and I, witnessed her enduring some of the most painful and debilitating asthma attacks – not fully understanding, or even having knowledge on how to treat the condition properly. After trying vapor rubs, steam therapy, and other naturopathic remedies, the Lord directed me to take her off of all dairy products, and anything with artificial sugars/sweeteners, whey, and unnatural products containing wheat or soy. During these very formative years of her life, the constant trauma the attacks caused on her body affected her thyroid, causing her to appear frail, weakly, and unable to gain weight. Nevertheless, thanks be to the God of Glory, that after implementing the new dietary regimen, her health greatly improved, the frequency of the asthma attacks decreased considerably, and she is now a strong, healthy, beautiful, active and successful adult!

Praise the Lord, from Whom ALL Blessings Flow!!

Miracle (19) –
The Thief Cometh...
But, God!

It was a very hot summer day, which ultimately turned into an extremely hot and humid, and just plain muggy night! In fact, as I recall, mostly every night that summer turned out the same. Moreover, being eight months pregnant at the time made the heat even more exhausting. As a result, we tried various methods to keep cool... from leaving fans running all day, to leaving the front and back doors open; to even lying on sheets on the floor... you name it! Well, on this particular evening, I chose to sit in our recliner and retire there for the rest of the night.

We weren't concerned about leaving both doors open at night (and never had been before), and let the night breeze circulate; but for some reason, the thought came to me to shut the back door. Well, I was too hot to move, and I was much too uncomfortable to even think about closing that door! Consequently, I sat there, but the thought entered my mind a second time; only this time, it was a little more intense. Even though the impression to move lingered in my spirit, I still did not attempt to close the door.

Thank God, because the next impulse to go and close the back door was so strong, that I could no longer resist! I literally jumped up, with the greatest sense of urgency, made my way to the back door, reached over the first flight of stairs, and slammed the door shut. My husband and I both wondered what on earth that was all about...especially questioning why I would do such a thing on one of the hottest nights of the season! Well, we soon found out what "*that*" turned out to be.

The following morning, as I headed down the back stairway, I could only gasp and praise the very God of Heaven, when I observed that someone had cut the screen (to the screen door), to pieces, and had actually managed to open it, jammed the lock, and left it wide open! Just imagine what could have happened had the main (all-steel) door not been closed! Thank God He sees all, knows all, and He is our Almighty Protector. It pays to know AND obey the voice (and leading) of the Lord – Hallelujah!!

Miracle (20) – Seven from Heaven!

Have you ever had the experience of planning something, and strangely, things don't always turn out the way you supposed they would? Such is the case with my first two daughters. My eldest (Marlena), was like a beautiful little baby doll. Before she was born, my husband and I thought sure we would name her after me, just as we had named our eldest son after him. As a matter of fact, this was his personal request! Nevertheless, once my first daughter was born, I was led to name her 'Marlena Elaine' (in memory of my husband's mother, Odessa Lena, whom he had lost three months prior to her birth). This decision was totally unplanned!

Well, after we found out that we were expecting another child, we both decided that if it were another girl, we would name her after me. Sure enough, we brought another daughter into the world! However, the very same thing happened again, and for some reason, I could not bring myself to name her after me! Instead, I decided to name her 'Rochelle Lanette,' after a fellow co-worker and former high school classmate. After expecting my seventh child, I wondered, "*now, is this supposed to be different?*" To my delight, it was! The moment I laid eyes on her…I knew it! Automatically, I felt led to name her after me…'Jacquelyn Renee' – although, I don't have a middle name, and the final syllable in my first name is spelled '-*LINE*' instead of '-*LYN*'. Now that she's an adult, all of her siblings remark that she is just like me— i.e., resemblance in our physical features, character traits, certain mannerisms, and in other distinct and unique expressions. She feels so special to be named after me and counts it a joy and blessing to be #7 (God's number of perfection). She thanks the Lord, and feels that's as close to a miracle as one can get!

Miracle (21) – Thank God for Her Deliverance!

I recall when my daughter, Lisa, the second to the youngest child, had a serious health scare. Because she is always on the go, busy focusing on and managing a very hectic schedule, she often has little time to attend to her health. Her strong desire to accomplish her goals eventually became a top priority, and I noticed that she seemed to be overextending herself and felt increasingly overwhelmed. Consequently, one morning, just as I was leaving my prayer room, on my way back downstairs, I heard a very loud thud.

Once I reached the landing of the stairwell and headed towards my bedroom, I saw my husband sitting on the edge of the bed with a perplexed and anxious look on his face. I immediately asked, *"What's wrong? Is something the matter?"* He replied, *"I think Lisa must have passed out…she's in the bathroom."* My heart jumped, and I hurried towards the bathroom door and tried to push it open. Then, I said, *"Lisa, let me in, open the door."* I tried to open it again, but I believed she was somewhat unconscious and may have been leaning against it, which prevented me from gaining access.

I finally pushed it open and pressed my way in, catching her in my arms just as she was about to collapse. I hastily walked her out of the bathroom, nearly dragging her through the living room towards the couch. She could barely speak and expressed that she felt faint and that she needed some air. Because her strength was nearly expended, I struggled to get her outside and quickly onto the porch. Once outside, I helped her to one of the lounge chairs, giving no regard for the bitter cold. At that moment, it didn't enter my mind to even grab our coats!

Her countenance changed and her skin began to turn pale (close to a grayish-white), and her lips were purple and parched. Even though it was cold outside, her hands were eerily cold. With the little strength she had, she clung tightly to me, and with her face buried in my stomach, she cried hysterically, saying, "*I can't see…it's so dark!*" She said she felt she was being pulled into another dimension. As I began to pray and intercede, I could hear her faintly pleading, "*I don't want to die…Lord, forgive me…whatever I've done…forgive me!*" I continued to lay hands on my daughter, holding onto her as tightly as I could, not releasing her until the Lord gave me the unction to do so.

Without hesitation, I immediately began to give God the Glory…Giving Him thanks and praising His Holy Name! Afterwards, I assisted her back inside, joyful to see her yet alive and functioning normally— without the aid/help of medical attention. Some hours later, my daughter, Jacquelyn, opted to take her to the hospital, where they expressed that she was severely dehydrated and had contracted a 24-hour stomach virus. Lisa soon admitted that she had been so busy tending to students at school, that she had often missed meals and wasn't drinking enough fluids.

Nevertheless, she desired to share this testimony in appreciation of my being there for her, and for praying and interceding on her behalf. She said that she is ultimately thankful to the Lord, realizing that, without a doubt, it was because of God's Mercy & Grace, coupled with the continued prayers of her Mother, that she is alive and well today! Bless His Awesome and Magnificent Name Forever!!

From the Author....

As a dedicated Evangelist and Servant of the Gospel of Christ, I appreciate and cherish the privilege to read God's precious Word, and I am thankful for possessing the God-given ability to minister and teach His powerful truth. The Father has blessed me with some of the greatest spiritual teachers and mentors, and I would be remiss in not honoring their legacy. To the precious sisters from my Senior Sunday School class, especially my previous teachers, who are all deceased, except for Sis. Isabelle Davis— who passed the mantle and anointed me as her successor— (Georgia Collins, Sis. Shelby, Rosetta Kay, Sis. Toy, Vera Ford), and students: (Noni Barnett, Ida Mae Canty, Jessie Edwards, Sadie Riser, Sis. Allen, Sis. McNeil, Lorraine Sawyer, and Edna Sawyer), who have also gone on to be with the Lord. I'm so thankful for how much they encouraged and appreciated me as their teacher.

I am also truly honored to have been called and anointed to help minister in the following capacities — Nursery Attendant, Artistic Designer for Married Women and Mother's Auxiliary, Artistic contributor for "Glory Magazine", Typist for "Apostolic Messenger of Truth Magazine", Herb Dresser, Choir Member, Witnessing and Canvassing Team, Vacation Bible School Teacher and Arts & Crafts Facilitator and Instructor, Baptismal Committee, Praying for and Visiting the Sick, Ministers Alliance Committee, Prayer Band Ministry, Sunday School Teacher (Adult and Seniors), and Follow-Up Committee Member.

Furthermore, I felt compelled to document my testimonies and share them with other believers, as well as with those who are seeking truth and deliverance, in the hopes that their faith and courage may be strengthened in the Lord. We are His eternal witnesses; commissioned to boldly proclaim the wonderful works of the Spirit. Because I am called, it is my duty to share the Power of God and to extend His hand of Grace and Mercy to everyone who will receive it.

Finally, this book fully represents a chronicle of my personal and intimate encounters of faith, hope, and deliverance, and reveals that God never fails and is true to His promises. It was my pleasure to share my journey of faith with you! My earnest prayer is that as you read each testimony, you were fully strengthened, and that your faith in God (now), is such that the Holy Spirit will reveal Himself to you and show Himself MIGHTY in your life as well!

To all of my fellow ministers, friends, and soldiers in Christ Jesus – thank you for your edification, steadfastness, fellowship, and faithfulness. Go forth in the Grace, Peace, and Love of the Only Wise and True God, through our Lord and Savior, Jesus Christ....for He is Worthy to be Praised!"

There is more...I simply can't tell it all! Thank you, Jesus!

Drawing is an artistic gift I inherited from my dad.

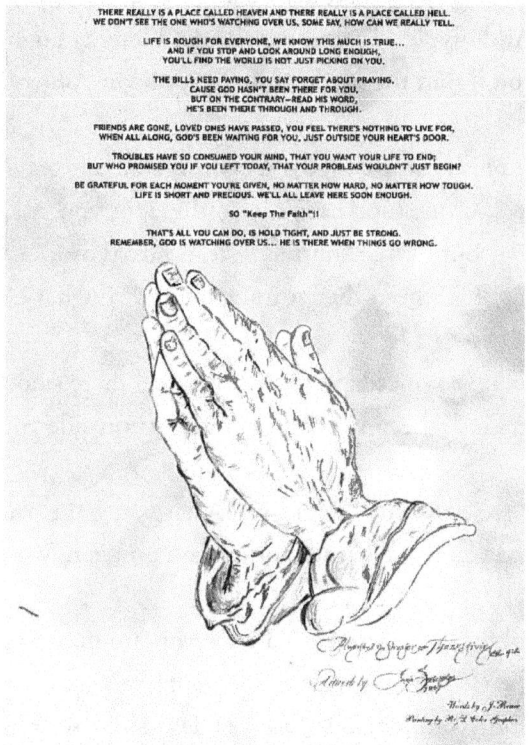

Artwork by Evangelist Jacqueline Stevenson - 1967
Poem *"Keep the Faith"* by Jacquelyn (J-Renee) Stevenson - 2005

(Full poem printed below)

KEEP THE FAITH

There really is a place called Heaven and there really is a place called Hell.
We don't see the One who's watching over us. Some say, how can we really tell?

Life is rough for everyone, we know this much is true…
And if you stop and look around long enough,
You'll find the world is not just picking on you.

The bills need paying, you say forget about praying,
Cause God hasn't been there for you,
But on the contrary – read His Word,
He's been there through and through.

Friends are gone, loved ones have passed, you feel there's nothing to live for,
When all along, God's been waiting for you, just outside your heart's door.

Troubles have so consumed your mind, that you want your life to end;
But who promised you if you left today, that you problems wouldn't just begin?

Be grateful for each moment you're given, no matter how hard,
no matter how tough.
Life is short and precious. We'll all leave here soon enough.

So "Keep the Faith"!!

That's all you can do, is hold tight, and just be strong.
Remember, God is watiching over us… He is there when things go wrong.

-Jacquelyn (J-Renee) Stevenson-2005

~END~

www.ingramcontent.com/pod-product-compliance
Lightning Source LLC
Chambersburg PA
CBHW052105070526
44584CB00017B/2343